SOCIAL CHALLENGES FACING CUBA

BY
DR. ANDY S. GOMEZ

authorHOUSE®

AuthorHouse™ LLC
1663 Liberty Drive
Bloomington, IN 47403
www.authorhouse.com
Phone: 1-800-839-8640

Published by AuthorHouse   04/30/2014

ISBN: 978-1-4918-7498-1 (sc)
ISBN: 978-1-4918-9800-0 (hc)
ISBN: 978-1-4918-7499-8 (e)

Library of Congress Control Number: 2014905269

CONTENTS

Chapter Three

Chapter Four

DEDICATION

I dedicate this book to my wife Frances for all the love, support and encouragement throughout the years. I also dedicate the book to the generation of my daughters and son in laws Frances Marie, Kristi Marie, Tony and Jose who I challenge to keep their Cuban history, culture and heritage alive for their children.

Finally, I dedicate the book to the memory of my father Andres and all those of his generation who have died in exile dreaming of returning to live in a free and democratic Cuba. Their dreams and fight for freedom will never be forgotten. The struggle shall continue until the tyranny of the Castro Brothers is defeated.

"It has been said that democracy is the worst form of government except all others that have been tried."

Sir Winston Churchill

PROLOGUE

I was born in Cuba on July, 1954. I spent my early childhood growing up in a middle class family in Havana. My family had everything we needed, own our home, good health, my father worked for Coca-Cola, private beach clubs and many other privileges Cuban society enjoyed during the 1950's. I attended private Catholic school and like many youngsters my age, we were not aware of the political instability our country found itself in.

On January 1, 1959 a new government led by Fidel Castro took power from Fulgencio Batista. I remember vividly the day Castro and his rebels marched into Havana on top of tanks and trucks wearing green fatigues with long beards and wearing rosaries around their necks. According to news reports I listened to, this was a "new beginning". A revolution intended to bring new hopes and a new political environment to our country. That all changed very quickly. In 1961 Fidel Castro declared that he was a Marxist-Leninist and that Cuba would become a communist nation.

On April 14, 1961 I left Cuba with my family running away from the fears of what Cuba might become. I was almost seven years old. When Castro nationalized all American companies including Coca-Cola, my dad along with most of the other administrators in the company were transfer to Caracas, Venezuela with the notion that Castro's government would not last very long and we would return to our homeland within six months. I remember that some of my parents friends did not open all their luggage.

The waiting kept getting longer each day that passed Castro's government got stronger. The days turned into months and the months turned into years. The hopes of going back to Cuba began to fade. It has been fifty-three years since I left Cuba and I'm still waiting for the government to collapse. By the late 1970's many in my parents generation began to loose hope of returning to Cuba. Going back became a nostalgic dream we lived each day in exile.

I grew up like many in my generation listening to stories our parents and grandparents told us about how wonderful Cuba was, " the paradise of the Caribbean." They left their futures behind. As a small child I could see the suffering on their faces every time Cuba was discussed. In many cases this sudden change in people's lives caused a psychological trauma that took time for many to recover from. My dad was transfer to Miami, Florida in 1964. They encountered a new culture, a new language, new value system that they had to adapt in order to start a new life and move on. Growing up I lived in two cultures. At home my Cuban culture was always present in the food we ate, the music we listened to and the stories about Cuba. Outside the home I was learning a new language but I was also developing a new set of values influenced by my schooling and my new friends. I began to assimilate into the American culture within years of arriving in the United States while my parents and grandparents struggled between both cultures and stories and dreams of the past.

I remember that each Christmas my father would propose a toast at the dinner table, " Next Year in Cuba", or New Year's Eve as the clock struck midnight we would bring in the new year singing the Cuban National Anthem. Just like the book by Professor Carlos Eire at Yale University, "Waiting for Snow in Havana", we are still waiting for the day we return to Cuba. I'm reminded of it each day when I look at a pillow my wife Frances gave me years ago that reads "El Proximo Ano Nuevo en la Habana." I keep that pillow in my living room to remind me of my father's dream and many like him who died wishing to return to Cuba.

When I graduated from high school, I was accepted at the University of Miami. Shortly thereafter I became very interested in learning more about Cuba and discovering more about my Cuban roots. I wanted to know what happened in 1959 and why it happened. I wanted to learn more about the Cuba before 1959. Today as a scholar of Cuba I have formed my own opinions and theories. I have traveled to Cuba twice, first in 2001, and then 2012 with the purpose of trying to learn more about what was going on in Cuba and how people were coping with the system.

The Cuba of today is very different to the Cuba my parents grew up in. The dreams of going back to that Cuba have for most part disappeared. Most in my parents and grandparents generation have died dreaming of going back. My generation and those of my children and grandchildren know very little about Cuba and most likely will never go back even if one day Cuba becomes free of the totalitarian regime its people have had to live and survive for over fifty-five years. The dream continues.

INTRODUCTION

On June 2001, I stepped down as Dean of the School of International Studies at the University of Miami and took a short sabbatical to do some research on Cuba. I wanted to use this time to learn more about what was taking place inside the island since the fall of the Soviet Union. My first goal was to return to Cuba to see for myself if the Cuba my parents and grandparents spoke about still existed. I wanted to see and experience first hand what the Cuban Revolution had accomplished and the impact the "Special Period" had on the Cuban people. The fall of the Soviet Union had stopped most of the economic support Cuba had been receiving from them since the early years of the revolution. The economic hardships brought about the "Special Period" had forced many Cubans to live a "Doble Moral" (double moral).

Once I arrived n Cuba, It did not take me very long to realize that the Cuba of the 1950"s was gone. The country had changed but also the people were very different than those I had grown up with in exile. They had first names that started with a "Y", they spoke words that I had never heard before. They spoke to me about how difficult it was to survive in Cuba each day not just economically but also psychologically. They spoke about the ideology of the revolution and how it emphasized the state over personal rights. Many individuals I spoke with were members of the Communist Party because it brought them some guarantees like the right to work or go to school not necessarily because they believed in the system. They had become a product of their surrounding environment mostly dominated by a "culture of fear" that manages their daily behaviors.

During my first trip to the island in 2001, I found the very elementary stages of a civil society. It was small, disorganized and basically made up of "Opositores" (opposition) to the regime. I found some small non-governmental organizations (NGO's) controlled by the government. There was very little space allowed for any type of serious opposition movement. I met many young people that had started to see and experience first hand the contradictions of an ideology they had learned in school full of empty promises. The trip was more educational than I expected. On the way back to Miami I kept asking myself where can you start to rebuild the values of a nation?

Shortly after arriving in Miami I decided that my next step would be to visit Central and Eastern Europe to see, learn, and experience how these countries were coping with breaking away from the Soviet Union and how their own transitions were progressing. My first stop was Hungary where I spent a great deal of time talking to the people particularly the young generation. I found a great deal of apathy for politics and a tremendous drive for improving their daily lives.

My second stop was the Czech Republic. I remember to this date sitting in the Czech Parliament and listening to the Prime Minister answering questions from reporters. One particularly young reporter asked him how he thought the transition plan of his government was going. The Prime Minister lowered his head for a minute and then spoke in a very somber voice and said, "If I had a chance to start over, I would have focused less on the politics and more on the needs of the people". He further explained that this would have helped build a stronger civil society that would have taken a bigger role in the changes the country was going through.

Within seconds, I realized that the answer to many of the problems countries in transition were facing had to do with the needs of the people above all else. The easier part for any country was to change the politics and economic system. To "change" people is the real challenge but where do you start? Familiarizing myself with the literature on government transitions, it clearly indicates that the most difficult part of any transition is to find ways on how to psychologically transform the human mind to support "change" after so many years living under totalitarian regimes. This makes it more difficult to develop and sustain a civil society that can support a vibrant democratic system in the future.

In my research I discovered that the word "change" has different meanings and implications according to each individual's personal experiences and surrounding environment. There have been hundreds of books written on Cuba since the start of the revolution. Most of these books talk about the fall of Fidel Castro and his regime. This book is not intended to examine in detail political and economic changes going on in Cuba. Instead, it will attempt to examine the psychological challenges facing the development and sustainability of a civil society on the island nation as well as an attempt to better understand the behavior of Cubans in order that one day a democratic government can be established and sustained.

At the same time, there is much that has been written on transitions of governments. One very good example is the reunification of Germany and the challenges and problems the government had to deal with. For example, the younger generation (18-35 years old) wanted change faster than the government could provide them. While the older generation (60 years plus) recognized the need for change, they were hesitant to embrace the idea completely in fear as to whether the changes would be positive or negative. This is called the "unknown factors." For example, after the reunification many former East Germans became nostalgic for how things were in the past. Not because they were better but instead because they had learned how to behave in the "box" that had been created by the regime. Now that the "box" or security blanket had been taken away, they had a hard time adjusting to the new social order. Many of them became nostalgic for the old ways. They had been conditioned how to function in the system.

Shortly after returning from Central and East Europe, I started to further my research trying to learn more about what had been written on the psychological trauma caused by "change" in these countries and the impact it had had on different age groups that had lived for long periods of time under totalitarian regime.

Most of the literature I found on transitions was about Russia, Poland, Czech Republic, Germany and other post-communist nations. The government transitions in these countries varied significantly. We must understand that there is no single model of "change" that can be applied one hundred percent to any nation including Cuba. Historical background, cultural values and personal experiences have a great deal to do with what might work or not. However, there are lessons that can be learned from their efforts. Defining what was needed first was not an easy process for the leaders in these countries. Applying another country's values and system will not work. What was very interesting was the fact that most of these countries used their educational system to begin to transform the values and attitudes of the young people in order to create a "new citizen." I will discuss later in the book how Cuba in the future can use their educational system to teach their citizens how to adapt to "change."

After six more months of studying the literature on the impact of government transitions on humans, I decided to form my own research team to see if we could begin to apply many of the concepts from other countries to Cuba. I reached out to psychiatrist, psychologist, sociologist, political scientist, and anthropologist that I knew from my years in higher education. This was a very important first step since my only formal training had been in education and politics. I did not want to start our research making the wrong assumptions or pretending I knew much about human behavior.

In 2002, I put the team together to start the project. After many long conversations and meetings, I invited Dr. Eugenio Rothe (MD, Psychiatrist at UM School of Medicine now at FIU School of Medicine) to be my Co-leader. Dr. Rothe had written extensively on this subject and had participated as a medical volunteer at the United States Guantanamo Base in Cuba during the "Balsero Crisis" of 1994. We also invited to join the team, Dr. Frank Mora (PhD, Political Scientist); Dr. Hector Palacios (MD, Psychiatrist recently arrived from Cuba); Dr. John Lewis (Ph.D, Research Methodologist); and Ramon Colas (Sociologist, Co-Founder of the Independent Library Movement in Cuba and a recent arrival from Cuba). We also had two consultants to the group. Dr Juan Clark (Ph.D, Sociologist, deceased 2013) and Hector Palacios, (Social Scientist and leading dissident in Cuba).

The group started to meet on a regular basis with the intent of developing a working plan and strategy that included writing a research proposal that would be submitted for approval to the University of Miami School of Medicine Institutional Review Board (IRB). In the proposal we indicated that we wanted to explore how can a nation and its people rebuild their value system after so many years living under a totalitarian regime? What challenges would be encountered by a new government in Cuba in creating a civil society? The research proposal included a survey that would be administer to Cubans on the island by trying to learn more about their experiences living under a totalitarian system of government and how this factor had shaped their behavior.

One of the primary research objectives of the survey was to try to understand the value orientations and opinions on issues pertaining to living in Cuba. We based our methodology on Kluckholm and Strodebeck (1963) designed to measure the value orientations of different cultures. They were the first researchers that designed such instrument of evaluation. We also used a questionnaire designed by Szapoeznik (1978),that tried to measure value orientations in exiled Cubans in Miami between 1960-1970. There were another important researchers that came before us such as Inclan (1985), and Santiesteban (2001) who used versions of the original research model to measure value orientations among other group of immigrants in the United States.

After many revisions to our original proposal, it was finally approved by the IRB six months after it had been submitted. This process was important because we wanted scientific approval for our study. We were now prepared to implement our plan.

The original plan called for sending the questionnaire to Hector Palacios in Havana who had developed a network of volunteers who would administer it throughout the island. However, in March of 2003 the "Black Spring" occurred in Cuba. The government imprisoned seventy-five leading dissidents including Hector Palacios. The Cuban government accused them of acting as agents of the United States. Our team now found ourselves with a plan and no way of implementing our survey in Cuba.

After a few months of debate and reflection, we decided that it would be a big risk to further try to administer the survey in Cuba. Instead, I approached the United States government and negotiated our entry way to recently arrived Cubans in the United States. These were Cubans that had arrived by boats or rafts on our shores or had crossed the Mexican frontier into the Southwest region of the United States predominantly Texas and were being process under the "Wet foot-Dry Foot Policy" of the United States.

We were given permission and access to these individuals that found themselves detained in the Krome Detention Center until being processed and released. We were allowed to interview them and administer our survey as part of their orientation. The data was collected and analyzed. The study was published and presented publicly in the fall of 2004. The results were received with tremendous interest by the academic community as well as by the Cuban-American community in South Florida. The results showed various degrees of trauma among the people we interviewed during the time they lived on the island.

Our research team disbanded shortly after the study was completed. However, I continued to study the impact totalitarian regimes have had on the way people behave after moving to a new place and living free. Since the original study, I have followed some of the individuals we studied and most of them suffered from some form of trauma such as separation from their families in Cuba. Many could not understand that being free brings a new set of responsibilities that they were not prepared for. Over the years I have continued to interview hundreds of recently arrived Cubans in South Florida and in Cuba during my trips with the goal of trying to better understand the impact "change" has on people and the trauma can be minimize.

Throughout the years I have also interviewed a small number of young Cubans residing in South Florida whose father, mother or close relative was or is a high ranking member of the Cuban government. Most claimed that they left Cuba because they could no longer support an ideology that has failed and the fact that Cuba offers very little hope for their futures.

In 2012, I was invited by the Catholic church to visit Cuba for Pope Benedict's visit. I used the opportunity to interview a large number of young Cubans allowing me to collect very valuable data on the "changes" that have taken place since Raul Castro took over for his ailing brother Fidel. I was particularly interested in learning more about the impact the "new reforms" have had on the individuals. This allowed me to compare the data collected in 2002 to 2012 in order to triangulate the findings and be able to increase the validity of the results.

During this trip I found more folks that spoke openly against the system of government. The dissident movement was still small and not well organized. The young people saw no hope for their futures and wanted to leave Cuba. One young lady told me "anywhere but Cuba." During the trip of 2012, I found that the level of frustration had increased from my original trip in 2001.

The purpose of this book is an attempt to introduce new concepts such as the "Human Factor" that must be taken into consideration during a transition of government. Some of these new ideas will require future research and studies by future scholars so that "change" can have a positive effect on human values and behaviors across all generations. I have also written this book for public policy makers so they can try to better understand that "change" from a totalitarian system of government to a so called democracy does not happen over night and will take time. Additionally, values and principles of democracy cannot be imported from other countries. It must be born within the people of Cuba.

The history of Cuba is rich and important. However, for the purpose of this book I will concentrate my analysis since 1990 or the start of the "Special Period" Finally, this book is not intended to answer all the questions a government in transition might encounter. It is more of a road map for everyone to think about so that new strategies can be developed, implemented and more importantly be sustained over the years.

CHAPTER ONE

EMERGENCE OF A CIVIL SOCIETY

CUBA IN THE 1990'S

The fall of the Soviet Union brought about an end to the economic support Cuba received from the communist nation (approximately $6.5 Billion). This brought about an economic crisis in Cuba known as the "Special Period" (Periodo Especial). One of the Cuban governments strategies to help them overcome the problem was to asked the Cuban people to make additional sacrifices in order to save the revolution (1). This strategy would help them find other allies that could come to their rescue.

The Cuban government economic plan called for the adjustment to the distribution of goods and services by giving equal access to the entire population to basic necessities such as food and shelter. These measures were received by the Cuban people with mixed reactions particularly by those members of the government that had been benefiting from the spoils of the system. For the first time, we begin to see resistance for "change" from the privilege members of society. Those at the bottom of the economic scale of society also began to question the new policies and whether they were willing to make more sacrifices for the revolution. These new economic changes brought about a high level of human suffering and anxieties as Cubans wondered how they would survive.

The economic crisis of the 1990's had a catastrophic impact on Cuban society. The "Special Period" can be divided into three parts:

(1) **Survival: 1990-1994.** This period began with the free fall of the economic conditions on the island; in a short period of time the gross domestic product dropped by 36%, consumption fell by 40% and the economy suffered unquantifiable losses of social capital. During this period, strategic contingency plans were implemented including emergency measures to counteract the plummeting energy supply and productive capacity. The deteriorating standards of living were devastating.

(2) **Slow Recovery: 1994-2001.** During this period, economic strategies introduced by the government consisted of adjustment policies, small measures to open up the economy and structural changes. Changes in the economic structure included a dollar-based monetary system; diversification of the forms and structures of ownership; and the emergence of parallel markets. One major change was driven by tourism. Cuban-Americans visiting the island or sending remittances to family and friends. This measure in particular began to create a high level of social inequality. Afro-Cubans who now made up approximately sixty percent of the population received very little support from outside Cuba where white Cuban-Americans in exile represented over ninety-five percent of the population. Other relevant institutional changes made by the government included administrative

decentralization of government functions, bank reforms, the creation of a commercial sector with foreign exchange, and some legal reforms. All these measures produced very limited results that helped alleviate the economic hardships. Between 1995—2001, the economy only grew by four percent. More importantly these changes by the government told Cubans for the first time since the start of the revolution not to count on the government for all their needs. The government would no longer be the primary supporter of the people.

(3) **Recession: 2001-2006.** The national economy began to show signs of recession. They included falling prices of raw materials, increased fuel and food costs, decline of tourism, and decline of direct investments. The liberalizing economic reforms proved to be too limited to have long everlasting effects. The recovery slowed down further to two-percent annually, delaying the goal of restoring the gross domestic product to 1989 levels. At the same time the governments social spending in programs such as healthcare and education declined significantly. During this period enrollment in higher education dropped fifteen percent indicative that young people did not see that getting an education could lead to a good job. These outcomes began to create a psychological level of hopelessness among Cuban society. During the recession period, unemployment reached as high as twenty percent while the government continued to grow at levels the economy could not support it.

During the 1990's, the social scenario in Cuba declined tremendously. There was an increase in crime, corruption, prostitution, drug trafficking, and illegal immigration. By 1995 it was estimated by the government that twenty-five percent of the population lived in poverty. In the late 1990's the Cuban population was approximately 11.2 million; of that total, 8.8 million had been born after the start of the revolution; and 2.2 million were born after the start of the "Special Period."

At the end of the 1990's we find a society in Cuba that is not what we scholars call a civil society. According to Professor Damian Fernandez, " what one found on the island was a proto-civil society somewhere between a defensive and emergent stage." (2) These groups were small with different identities and interests. For example, in 1987 Oswaldo Paya's Christian Liberation Movement was born along with the Independent Library Movement Co-founded by Ramon Colas and his ex-wife Berta Mixor and a number of human rights groups.

As the state's economic reforms put additional pressures on society, the government started to loose some control of what Professor Fernandez called "La Calle" (the streets) (3). This opened up space for additional and alternative groups to form with the primary purpose of seeking new sources of economic welfare and a personal identity outside the official channels. It is during this period that the term "Doble Moral" (Double Moral) is born. Professor Jose Azel describes this concept in his book *Mañana in Cuba* as a "form of dual morality where one standard of conduct applies to the public sphere and a different one applies to the private conduct of the individual." (4)

DEFINING CIVIL SOCIETY

Throughout the years I have discovered that the term civil society has multiple meanings and many times it is misused by scholars and policy makers alike. I argue that the term civil society has two basic meanings, first as an analytical category, and second as a movement that creates political activism.

Civil society can be defined as the realm of public groups and associations created for the purpose of articulating or representing individual or group interests. It plays an intermediary role between individual and family interests and the state as well as other actors. As such, it cannot be understood in isolation from other elements of polity. (5) It is very important to understand that the presence or absence of a civil society is dependent to the level of development and nature of the political regime.

According to Professor Juan Carlos Espinosa, "societies are born from the increasing complexity of social and economic life and the proliferation of interests, identities and causes." (6) Therefore, a particular civil society is the result of unique combinations of structures, cultures, values, and notions of public versus private. For example, we cannot put in the same category the emergence of civil societies in Post-Soviet States, the "Arab Spring" or those in other parts of the world. Each development is quite unique. As Anthony Smith explained in his classic, *The Ethnic Origins of Nations,* what distinguishes ethnic communities from other groups are a collective name, a common myth of descent, a shared history, a distinctive culture, an association with a specific territory, and a sense of solidarity with each other. (7)

PRECONDITIONS FOR THE EMERGENCE OF A CIVIL SOCIETY

Weigle and Buttefield (1992) concluded that the seeds of civil society sprouted in Central and Eastern Europe as a result of a systemic crisis brought about "the failure of the regimes to adequately perform clearly defined functions and the failure of the regimes to efficiently respond to the basic needs of society." (8)

Weigle and Butterfield go on to describe four stages in the development of a civil society that can be applied anywhere. they are:

(1) **Defensive**: Private individuals and independent groups actively or passively defend their autonomy from the party-state,

(2) **Emergent:** Independent social groups or movements seek limited goals in a widened public sphere sanctioned by the party-state.

(3) **Mobilization**: Independent groups or movements undermine the legitimacy of the party-state offering alternative forms of governance to a politicized society.

(4) **Institutional**: Publicly supported leaders enact laws guaranteeing autonomy of social action, leading to an agreement between the state and society with the ultimate goal of having free elections.

When analyzing these stages, we can say that the first two stages (Defensive and Emergent) are shaped by the characteristics of the existing regime, while the last two (Mobilization and Institutional) depend largely on historical precedent, political culture, nationalism, and the level of institutional development in the country. In order to understand how the process starts, we must examine the nature of the regime, the severity of the systemic crisis, the capabilities (or lack) of the state, the status of social initiative, the political culture, and finally the historical trajectory of the country.

The most important preconditions for the emergence of a civil society are the survival of independent thought and of some patterns of social organization. In the case of Cuba, the communist regime eliminated the opposition from the early stages of the revolution and dissolved independent sources of power that could rival the communist party such as other political parties, trade unions, professional organizations, religious organizations, as well as any other possible threat to their control of power.

Pre-1960 non-communist organizations were banned, co-opted, or merged into new entities created by the state. For example, the creation of the Federation of Cuban Women, founded in 1960 by Vilma Espin (1930-2007) former wife of Raul Castro served as its president until her death. Prior to 1960, there were over 1,000 women's groups on the island. While the majority of the population were inducted (voluntary or not) into mass organizations that served as "Voceros" (Voices) for the party and state. Alternative visions and ideas that differed from the state disappeared or went "underground", or into exile.

According to Ariel Hidalgo, " The social contradictions repressed by all means will, by necessity, emerge later illegally. Despite the rigid totalitarian structure, the emergence of parallel trade unions, human rights committees, and independent cultural and religious associations is inevitable (9). Hidalgo is referring to what we have seen in Cuba since the late 1980's and early 1990's which is the emergence of dissident, opposition and independent social organizations.

Starting with the late 1980's, the Cuban government had to take a number of measures with some of the ideological challenges the regime was facing. Unlike the "New Russia", and other of its former satellite nations, Cuba's respond to "Glasnot and Perestroika" was to resist any type of political change. Fidel Castro made it very clear that Cuba would not follow the pattern of changes taking place in Central and Eastern Europe.

However, by 1992-1994 it was clear that the Cuban government's limited economic reforms were not going to be enough to meet society's needs. The government's response was to utilize the "exile option", the exportation of opposition leaders and others that were discontent to other countries. This led to the "Balsero Crisis" of 1994. It was a way of decapitating the emergence of a civil society. This strategy had been used before. First in 1965 with the "Camarioca Boatlift," and later the "Mariel Boatlift" in 1980. Weigle (1991) referred to this process as "decompression." (10) A way by which any government allows some pressure of daily life to escape.

By 1995 we find that many new organizations had flourished on the island. During this period of activism, we can divide social life into three parts: (1) Socialist civil society; (2) Alternative civil society; and (3) Informal civil society. The defining characteristics for all three groups are the relationship with the party-state. A relationship that has limited conflict within its boundaries of operation. This leniency on the part of the Cuban government is carefully monitor by the political and security apparatus. The kind of behavior and practices allowed were quite limited.

EMERGENCE OF A CIVIL SOCIETY

One can argue that the "Special Period" was not just an economic crisis. According to Professor Rafael Hernandez, editor of the Cuban Magazine *Temas* and a leading intellectual on the island, after the "Special Period" "Cuba passed from Socialism A to Socialism B" (11) The plan was to create a less state-centered model of Socialism all mandated by the economic hardships of the period.

The transformation of Cuban society started in the 1980's when Cubans in general began to loose faith in the ideology they had been indoctrinated. This was compounded by the decline of living standards as well. It was during this period that we begin to see the government open up more space for debate on the issues affecting society in general.

The socialist renewal that took place in Cuba had vey different characteristics than those that took place in the old Soviet Union. For example, "Perestroika and Glasnot" began as reform policies that eventually gave rise to properly anti-socialist sectors. The Castro brothers understood very clear that they could loose control and while they were willing to entertain ideas for reforms, this would not change the system.

The emergence of civil society in Cuba during this period had similar characteristics of those in Russia and other parts of Central and Eastern Europe. However, if we apply Weigle's and Butterfield's theory, we can argue that even today Cuba's civil society is in the defensive stage. The Cuban case exhibits an old amalgam of elements that by society coexisting, it calls into question the relationship between an emerging civil society and the hopes of a democratic transition in the future. Yet some of the characteristics that would define a passage into the "emergent" state appeared in 1991 when the communist party changed its attitudes towards religious practices by allowing believers in God to join the communist party.

The independent civic movement started with the state authorizing the creation of the first Non-Governmental Organization (NGO) in 1992. The Centro Felix Varela led a boom of new NGO's between 1992—1996. It did not take long for everyone to learn that these NGO's were part of the state apparatus. They became known as "Gongos". Government Controlled Organizations.

The real independent civic movement started tentatively in Cuba in the mid-1990"s with the formation of various independent professional organizations and more importantly with the emergence of the independent journalist movement led by Raul Rivero who created the first independent Cuban Press Agency. Some 135 of these groups came together in October 1995 to form the Concilio Cubano; an umbrella organization that declared its determination to struggle for an absolutely peaceful and non violent transition in Cuba to a democratic state of law. The Concilio Cubano plans to hold a meeting on February 24, 1996 were blocked by the Cuban regime, which arrested many of the leading activists, labeling all in the group to be "counter revolutionaries" created and funded by the US Central Intelligence Agency (CIA) and the "Miami Mafia" often referred to the Cubans living in South Florida. The movement showed persistence and resilience despite continued repression. Today, its leader Raul Rivero lives in exile in Madrid, Spain.

Another example of this new civil society in Cuba was the birth of the Independent Library Movement Co-Founded by Ramon Colas and his former wife Berta Mexidor both Afro-Cubans from Las Tunas. They started by establishing a library of books in their house for their neighbors to read. Colas and Mexidor encouraged others across the island to join the movement in-order to provide Cubans uncensored access to literature and information they had not seen or heard before. At its peak the movement had 130 libraries all over the island with an estimated quarter of a million patrons. After hearing of the movement, Fidel Castro declared at an International Book Fair in Havana, that " there were no banned books and magazines in Cuba, only the lack of funds to purchase them." (12) Colas and his family were forced into exile. Today Ramon Colas lives in Jackson, Mississippi and the libraries in Cuba have slowly disappeared due to lack of funds and support.

The new civic movement brought many groups together for the first time. All with one common goal, changing the government. The movement included Catholics, Protestants, revolutionaries, democratic socialist, constitutionalists, members of the pre-1959 political parties as the "Autenticos and Ortodoxos". In addition you found farmers, students, and workers at all levels, and even some entrepreneurs working on government owned micro-enterprises that the government had made legal during the "Special Period." The common denominator that united all these groups and individuals was the core principle of wanting freedom. We can trace their main concept back to the 18th century "Independentistas" thought that the state's legitimacy beginnings with the people, and that the government's mandate from the people should be to protect its citizens natural rights. The tough question we ask ourselves is, can the Cuban government erase fifty-five years of totalitarianism including the indoctrination of a Marxist ideology and transition to a more open government? Probably not overnight.

A group that is worth talking more about is the Christian Liberation Movement (CLM) founded by the late Oswaldo Paya. Paya was not part of the traditional anti-Castro opposition, but rather he belonged to a new generation of Catholic activists who opposed the

Castro dictatorship. In fact, Paya did not consider himself a political dissident but rather an individual who drew his inspiration from the social teachings of the Catholic church and the writings of Father Felix Varela (1788-1853). Varela was the Catholic priest who started an intellectual and moral movement for Cuban independence. During Pope John Paul II's visit to Cuba in 1998, the Pope called Father Varela "the foundation stone of the Cuban national identity (13).

Encouraged by the Pope's visit to Cuba, Paya founded the "Proyecto Varela" with the purpose of bringing greater freedom to Cuba. Paya attempted to amend the Cuban constitution but at the end it was rejected by the Cuban National Assembly even after he collected the necessary signatures required. The "Proyecto Varela" became an international symbol of the Cuban people struggles for freedom.

Another sign of repression by the Cuban government came on March 18, 2003, when the Cuban government arrested seventy-five of the leading dissidents including twenty-five members of the Varela Project. This act by the Cuban government became known as "The Black Spring." These actions by the government energized many people on the island who continued to protest demanding freedom. One such group are the "Damas de Blanco" (Ladies in White). They are the wives of the men who were imprisoned during the "Black Spring." The group started to meet every Sunday at St. Rita's Catholic Church in Havana. The group marches after mass through the streets of Havana demanding their freedom. These lady's all dress in white and come from all sectors of society. Their practices continue today under tremendous pressure from the government and severe repression. Their founding member Laura Pollan died several years ago under the suspicion that she was poisoned by the government while recuperating from an ailment in a hospital in

Havana. An Afro-Cuban and very strong leader by the name of Berta Soler heads the group today.

In addition to the increased government activities of oppression during the 1990's, Young Cubans began to form grass-root groups in their neighborhoods with the purpose of expressing themselves about what they did not like with the current system of government. These meetings were informal, self-organized and very spontaneous. For example, it is during this time that Cuban bloggers like Yoani Sanchez began to post blogs with very limited access about the daily life and events on the island from an independent perspective. These blogs raised the level awareness about Cubans struggles for freedom across the world.

Another example of this new young opposition was the underground rock music movement. Independent rock bands began to write lyrics and sing songs that were highly critical of the regime and its policies. These groups emerged throughout the island giving illegal concerts in abandoned theaters, cafes or even private homes. The most famous of these groups was led by a young punk artist named Gorky Aguila who wrote a song entitled, " Porno Para Ricardo" very critical of the Cuban government. Gorky was arrested in 2003 for his actions. While in, prison Gorky had the opportunity to meet with many imprisoned dissidents. One individual that caught his attention was an Afro-Cuban named Dr. Oscar Elias Biscet. Gorky credits Dr. Biscet for giving him the inspiration and strength to continue his fight against the regime. Upon Gorky's release from jail he wrote, " I've lost my fear, I've already been a prisoner and face the darkness of the Castro's dictatorship" (14) Gorky became an international symbol for writers and musicians that for the first time took up the call for asking freedom in Cuba.

The opposition in Cuba has not been a vertical centralized movement. It is more like a horizontal patchwork of ideas that has created an independent civic movement. It is not leaderless but is is multipolar and it has multiple levels of interest. It is highly decentralized and has an organizational structure that allows the movement to survive government organized campaigns of repression and subversion. Because the movement is not particularly hierarchical, the regime's normal tactics of trying to infiltrate their ranks has not been able to completely shut it down. Even if a large number of people are arrested, the civic movement is diverse enough to carry on. A key challenge to the movement faces each day is their ability to communicate with each other across the island. The Cuban government historically has been able to control all modes of communication. What we saw in Egypt and other countries in North Africa or the Middleast during the "Arab Spring" would be very difficult to replicate in Cuba. The use of cell phones and internet services are not readily accessible across the island,

The expansion of the Cuban civic movement has raised many levels of concerns for the regime since the 1990's. A year before Fidel Castro retired as Cuba's leader, he called on the Cuban people to commit acts of repudiation against pro-democracy protests and their leadership. As these acts of repudiation increased across the island, the civic movement demonstrated great resilience in its tactics by organizing a non-cooperation campaign across the island. A good example of this campaign occurred in October of 2007 when the Cuban National Assembly was about to ratify Raul Castro as the country's President and about 1.4 million Cubans did not vote. Up to that moment the regime had gone to extreme measures to get the entire population to vote. This was the largest non-votes casted in any election in Cuba. It was a clear sign that there was a respectable number of Cubans that wanted "change."

This campaign of non-cooperation was focused on three groups of Cuban society that had been marginalized by the regime. The young people, the Afro-Cubans, and the poor. According to Professor Damian Fernandez, "The young people still constitutes the single most potentially explosive social group for the regime and its successors." (15) Professor Fernandez is referring mostly to what he calls the "de-socialized and marginal youth, the dropouts, the jobless who make up three-quarters of Cuba's unemployed, and in addition those who have been drawn to drugs, crime and prostitution. The youth are frustrated and see no hope for the future. These frustrations and anger are demonstrated in the lyrics of rock musicians. Even the elite youth including sons and daughters of members of the regime see the sharp contradictions between the official ideology and the harsh hypocrisy they live each day." (16) As the son of a high ranking member of Cuba's government told me in an interview, " I was a Prince of the revolution and at the same time I was a prisoner of it." (17).

The other two groups are the Afro-Cubans (including Mulatos) who make-up sixty-five percent of the population and the poor who according to the Cuban government they represent twenty-five percent of the population. In reality that number is much higher yet very difficult to assess since most of the population receives $20 per month. Those that are retired have had a very difficult time as well since their monthly pensions have been reduced significantly. Since the large percentage of Cuba's immigration has been mostly white, the Afro-Cubans are less likely to receive financial support from abroad. The Cuban Revolution had promised the Afro-Cuban population more equality. However, they are rarely seen in positions of power within the government or good jobs with very few exceptions. For example, in the tourism industry controlled by the government, white managers often insist that prospective employees conform to standards that are interpreted to exclude Afro-Cubans. Many of them have been forced to seek informal work or migrate to urban areas of the country looking for better opportunities. If caught by the government, they are often return to their home cities which highlights a growing racial tension in Cuba.

Therefore, it should not be surprising that the civic resistance movement has become very active in the non-white providences where we find some of the current leaders of the opposition such as Dr. Oscar Elias Biscet, Jorge Luis Garcia Perez better known as "Antunez" and Guillermo Farinas. What is interesting is how the protests transcend race in favor of addressing the plight of all oppressed Cubans.

The case of "Antunez" is very interesting. During his long-term in jail (he was released in 2007 and apprehended for short periods of time since then), his fellow inmates came to call him "The Black Diamond" because of his courage and unbreakable spirit. "Antunez" has acknowledged that racism played a role in his own oppression. According to an interview "Antunez" gave an international reporter in Cuba after his release in 2007, he said that "the Cuban authorities never tolerated that a black person could dare to oppose the regime. During the trial, the color of my skin aggravated the situation. Later when I was mistreated in prison by the Cuban guards' they always referred to me as being black." (18). This is a value set and pattern of behavior that is found in Cuban society today.

CONCLUSION

In terms of Weigle and Butterfield's model, Cuba's emerging civil society is still in the "Defensive" Stage." (19) As mentioned earlier in this chapter, the situation in Cuba is quite complex. The Cuban case exhibits an odd set of variables and elements that by coexisting, it calls into question the relationship between the civil society and the government of Raul Castro. Some of the characteristics that would define a passage of the current movement to an "Emergent Stage" appeared briefly in 1991 when the communist party allowed so called "believers" to join the party. Another step was taken when the state authorized the creation of non-governmental organizations in 1992. However, all along the government had no intention of loosing control of their activities.

When the regime legalized the use and possession of hard currency "dollarization", limited self-employment, farmer's cooperatives, and artisan shops started to open mostly catering to the tourist with very limited domestic consumption. However, the possibility of earning an income from non-state resources became very attractive to most Cubans. The limited economic reforms introduced by the government have not created enough consumer demand or put money in the hands of most Cubans to keep many of these shops and stores open.

These developments have continued to be permissible by the government while organizations opposing the regime continue to be harassed and many of the leaders of this so called civil society continue to be jailed or expelled from the country. There was also a brief thaw immediately before and after the visits of both Pope's (1998 and 2012). However, the crackdown of 1996 that led to the jailing of activists, the intensification of ideological war by the draconian " Law for the Protection of National Sovereignty" (1999). This was a clear indication that the regime would continue to reject any vision different then their own and further control the development of a growing civil society. Other than the limited debates on economic reforms in 1993—1994 in the National Assembly, there was no public evidence of intra-party debates and no space was opened for many of these new organizations and opposition groups. There were no additional steps taken to allow freedom of speech. On the contrary, there was further retrenchment and an intensification of the government campaign to discredit any opposition.

In 1988, Cuba actually had a larger and more active dissident and opposition movement than many of the regimes that collapsed when the Soviet Union reformed its political system. Although Cuba survived the "Leninist Extinction", the Castro government did not become a "reformist" regime that would allow a civil society to pass from a "Defensive Stage" to an "Emergent Stage." Instead, the regime has slowly eroded, along with the state's capabilities, its legitimacy, and it continues on a path today of a hybrid of Stalinism. The regime under Raul Castro has been able to maintain elite loyalty and renegotiate the coercive methods sufficiently to stave off a revolt from below or the emergence of a large social movement that would coalesce any type of political opposition. However, the question remains how long can the regime provide minimum support to keep the Cuban people in check. The government fully understands the dangers of reform and it also understands that to accept the legitimacy of an opposition and allow independent social activism to compete for the hearts and minds of the Cuban people could mean the end to their political control.

CHAPTER TWO

HOW CUBANS THINK

BACKGROUND

The people that have lived under totalitarian regimes have had to learn to survive within a "culture of fear." Like the people in Cuba today, they have developed a set of values and attitudes that defines their daily behavior in order to align their own wants and needs to the restrictions imposed by the state. It is that "culture of fear" that has dominated Cuban society for over fifty-five years that future policy makers on the island will have to take into consideration when real change is introduced.

Hughes (1993) defines "culture" into five key variables; (1) a society transmitted system of ideas; (2) something that shapes and describes experience; (3) it gives names to the surrounding reality; (4) is shared by members of a particular group, and (5) coordinates and determines human behavior. (20). Hughes defines the "culture process" as a means of conveying values across generations. (21)

Culture in turn, develops a system of social values which are defined as the ideals, customs, and institutions of a society. These are: (1) deeply influenced by the surrounding reality, (2) they can vary from one culture to another, and (3) they can change over time. For example, they are passed from one generation to another and each generation adapts to new and different realities and survival skills (Hughes, 1976; 1993).

For Cubans there are two major cultural groups that have evolved over the past fifty-five years. The Cuban community on the island and the Cuban community in exile. Each cultural group has faced and adapted to dramatically different historical and environmental circumstances. The most notable circumstance has been that Cubans on the island have been indoctrinated to believe in their Marxist-Leninist ideology, whereas Cuban who immigrated to the United States and other places around the world for most part have lived in a capitalistic, democratic, free market system of government.

Kluckhohn and Strodbeck (1963) were the first researchers that designed a validated instrument with the purpose of measuring value orientations. They measured the value orientations of the members of different cultures focusing on five primary domains. These are: (1) how the individual understands the character of human nature (good vs. evil), (2) How the individual relates to authority (paternalistic vs. egalitarian versus individualistic); how the individual orients himself/herself with respect to time (traditions-past versus present versus future), (4) how the individual chooses to use activity (pleasure versus ambition versus spirituality), and (5) how the individual relates to nature. (22) Their work has served as a model to many social scientist including myself trying to learn how people behave in certain circumstances.

One of the results of the Cuban Revolution of 1959 has been the fragmentation of the Cuban community and Cuban family. The "Cuban Diaspora" has continued without any major interruptions since 1959. Many Cubans of both sides of the Florida Straits have placed their hopes on a future reunification similar to the German experience. The systematic understanding of the differences in value orientations among the members of the Cuban community on the island and those in exile will constitute a cornerstone in the planning and implementation of a process between both groups who after fifty-five years have developed very distinct set of values.

Since the collapse of the Soviet Union in 1991, many changes have taken place inside Cuba. For one, Fidel Castro is no longer in charge of the government. The dissident and opposition movement has continued to slowly grow within the space permitted by the state. Many of its leaders have been allowed to travel outside the island for the first time bringing different voices of hopes with similar messages to the exile community in South Florida. One particular message that struck me was mentioned in a speech by Cuba's famous blogger Yoani Sanchez. She said, "I found a Cuba outside Cuba" (23). However, when you sit down with her and other of these individuals, you realize how much living in a totalitarian system for so long has shaped how they think and what they say. At the same time the attitudes of the Cuban-American community in exile has also changed over the years. Even though we are tied by history and culture, our value system and attitudes have been shaped by the American system

COMPARATIVE VALUE ORIENTATIONS DURING TRANSITIONS

The transition from a totalitarian regime to a democratic society has proven to be a very complex sociopolitical and psychological process for those individuals from Central and Eastern Europe. For example, the communist way of life offered predictability and safety, which can be abruptly lifted during a transition. Such changes can also cause psychological trauma when dealing with the "unknown factors" that change brings. Passing responsibility from the state to the individual can be confusing and traumatic. In addition, sharp generational differences will exist during any transition. The elderly usually will become nostalgic during the process of change and will want to return to the "old ways" not because they were better but because they fear "change" and know how to behave within "the box." The middle generation defined as those who lived their childhood and adolescence under communism and are now adults and possibly the most politically active with struggle with the uncertainty about their future and the slowness of the reforms. Psychologically they are caught between two value systems. Those of the past as children and those of the present as adults. Finally, the younger generation, who have very limited memory of communism become socialized during a period of restructuring when values are fluid and seem to believe and trust nothing. There lives are ruled by wanting change faster than a transition government can provide. They can also develop antisocial patterns of behavior that are counterproductive to "change."

Smith (1999) studied different reactions to transition among Russians of different ages. Smith emphasized in his study the importance of the "psychological dimension" of political transitions and quotes the former Soviet President Mikahel Gorvachev"s dictum that for a political transition of a country to take place, a great deal of emphasis must be put on the needs of the people (Smith, 1999) (24). These are:

BASIC NEEDS

Safety
Food
Housing
Jobs
Transportation
Education/Training
Healthcare

Smith (1999) developed a six step model to try to explain the psychological stages that citizens undergo during a government transition. They are: (1) braking down the legitimate values of the old regime; (2) mobilization; (3) de-institutionalization or purge; (4) romantic reforms that are institution building; (5) institutional failure that leads to social reaction and retrenchment; and (6) consolidation and redefinition of the course and pace of the reforms. He further divided each stage into five areas covering (1) the political system; (2) the economy; (3) social level; (4) psychological level; and (5) the ethnic regional and cultural level.

This model developed by Smith was intended to better understand the transition of Russia out of communism. However, in spite of the commonalities that exist among all humans beings, we must understand that this model may not completely apply to Cuba given the significant differences in culture, history and environmental factors surrounding each society's experiences.

Shiraev (1999) highlighted the psychological difficulties that many Russians encountered during their transition. A key factor was the willingness on the part of the Russians " to give up certain civil liberties in order to recover the previous stability and safety that existed under communism." (25). This concept is explained by Ian Brenner book "The J Curve." Brenner argued that for a country that is stable because is closed to become a country that is stable because it is open, it must go through a transitional period of dangerous instability.

EARLY STAGES

Wieckzorkowska and Burnstein (2001) designed a classification of two psychological typologies and how these two different groups of individuals adapt to "change" during a government transition. The two classifications are: "(1) Point Strategist who are individuals more focused, tenacious in their pursuit of goals. (2) Interval Strategist who are individuals better suited to adapt and survive under a totalitarian system, where the options are limited and the opportunities for improvement are scarce and sporadic." (27)

Wooden and collaborators (2002) attempted to study the attitudes of Cuban youth living on the island trying to find out how these youngsters were affected by the collapse of the Soviet Bloc. They conducted a survey in Cuba randomly approaching people on the streets. The sample consisted of seventy Cubans from the ages of 14 to 29 years old. The results of their study were compromised since the investigators did not take into consideration the repressive nature of the Cuban regime which precluded any individual to answer the questions openly formulated by a stranger they did not know. (28)

Inkeles and Bauer (1968) faced a similar dilemma in 1951, when they attempted to study the Soviet system at the height of the cold war. In what became known as the "Harvard Project on the Soviet Social System." These investigators interviewed individuals that were within days of having crossed the "Iron Curtain" into Western Europe. They formulated the interview by reminding their subjects to answer the questions as if they were still living in the "Soviet Bloc."(29)

Roberts (1999) conducted a survey on recently arrived Cubans in South Florida and this study became very valuable for advancing the sampling methods for assessing the behavior of immigrants. Roberts and his team of researchers studied the immigrants opinions regarding seven key variables. These were: (1) Remittances of money by relatives and humanitarian aid to Cuba by the United States, relatives or friends; (2) Human rights and incarceration of dissidents: (3) Opinions on the education and healthcare systems in Cuba; (4) The Cuban media and modes of certain information, (5) Reaction to young and old political leaders; (6) Moral values and the Catholic church; and (7) Opinions regarding the future political transition of the country.(30)

Roberts and his team were also interested in measuring the mood of the Cuban people as a result of the collapse of communism in the former Soviet Union and the change of United States policy towards Cuba. The purpose of their study was to assess the impact these factors had on an emerging civil society in Cuba and to try to better understand their viewpoints on Cuban society. Some of the most important findings of the Roberts' study included: (1) Enrollment in higher education had declined by over thirty percent with members of the younger generation choosing to work for the tourist industry or leave the country; (2) The respondents reported some satisfaction with the improvements of the healthcare system; (3) The majority of the respondents rejected the Cuban government's propaganda that blamed the United States Economic Embargo on the financial problems on the island; (4) Most of those individuals interviewed were unaware of the activities of the political dissidents; (5) The perception of the Cuban government leadership was very negative; and (6) Overwhelming majority supported the idea of a transition to democracy. (31)

2002 STUDY RESULTS

BACKGROUND

Let us now analyze the results of the study my team of researchers put together to better understand how Cubans think today inside the island. The sample of recently arrived Cubans that were administered the survey and were interviewed was 304 with 62% being male and 37% female. One individual did not list his gender. The average age of the group was thirty-four years old, 57% consider themselves poor while 54% claimed to have children. Finally, 46% claimed to have some type of education.

VALUE ORIENTATIONS

To measure the value orientations and opinions of recently arrived Cubans, we matched the domains of man's relationship to (1) Time, (2) Authority, (3) Human Nature, and (4) Activity. This methodology was adapted from earlier studies conducted by Kluckhorn and Strobeck in 1963 and modified by Szapoeznik in 1978 and Santiesteban in 2001. Each section of the study provided the individual being interviewed with a scenario and options on how they would deal with in a particular situation.

ORIENTATION: MAN VERSUS TIME

The communist influence on the island of Cuba over the past fifty-five years may account for the fact that only 21% of those individuals in our research chose to raise their children according to past traditions. Pre-revolutionary society and traditions (past oriented) vilified in the decade of the 1960's and 1970's, and considered to be negative and Counter-revolutionary. They were strongly discouraged, especially during the first two decades of the Cuban Revolution. Taking into account the difficult financial situation that followed the collapse of the Soviet Union, which forced Cubans to survive one day at a time, iI would have been expected that the majority of the responses would have been to prepare their children to survive in the present (present oriented). The majority of the individuals surveyed (52%) responded that they would raise their children by preparing them for a better future (future oriented). These values seem to be more in keeping with the values of immigrants around the world, and perhaps it explains why people choose to immigrate from Cuba in the first place, given the poor economic conditions and limited opportunities for the future.

A seemingly contradictory connection to this point was that individuals that classified themselves as poor (54%) chose the reason to leave Cuba as "future orientation" more than those in the middle and upper middle class (49%) according to 2002 statistics of the Cuban government. Individuals of the lower (poor) social classes of most countries are often plagued by socio-economic inequities and are oppressed by poverty. This precludes them from planning for the future, and instead forces them to employ their energy and focus on surviving each day. Planning for the future is a luxury that is usually afforded to those whose basic needs have already been met (Inclan, 1985).

In our study, we ventured to speculate that the reason for this contradiction may be explained by the fact that in Cuba, individuals of the poor social class are more deeply affected by the present financial crisis than those in the middle and upper middle classes, who are more likely to be part of the status quo and of the groups that hold the economic and political power on the island. Therefore, they are more sheltered from distress and less likely to feel that they are facing a dead end without possibilities of improvement if they stay in Cuba.

Another interesting finding was that those individuals with a higher level of education (78%), chose to prepare their children for the future and thus, are more future oriented than those with lower levels of education (49%). This finding is similar to what would be expected among individuals of the United States middle class, or members of the middle class of any other country in the world possessing similar levels of education. This future-orientation found in the majority (52%) of those individuals in our study, represents a good fit with the values of the American middle class and those Cubans who immigrated to the United States in the early 1960's and could serve as a predictor of socio-economic success and acculturation among the new arrivals.

MEANING OF LIFE

In this section of our survey, the individuals were asked what he or she would like to do with their free time. Traditionally, people of Hispanic origin choose to spend their free time enjoying the company of their families and friends. This is explained by the culture's emphasis on the centrality of the family, and the individual's life-long affiliations with his or her extended family network system. The style of relating to others is known as "Personalismo", where the individual places trust and prefers to form affiliations with particular group of individuals rather than institutions or organizations (Bernal 1982, Ruiz 2001).

Surprisingly, the majority of our sample (53%) responded that they would prefer to spend their time trying to get as far as they could in life. Again, this value orientation may be more representative in immigrants who separate themselves from the average individual as a result of their ambition, motivation, and desire for a better future. Immigrants tend to be "goal oriented" and 'future oriented." We can also speculate that those individuals who are more spiritual and self-reflective may be able to spend more time in their "inner world" and may be able to find shelter from oppressing conditions outside themselves, making them more able to tolerate external "material" frustrations and therefore, less likely to immigrate. Ultimately, it is important to consider that the Cuban government created a "police state" on the island, where friends and even members of your family cannot be trusted. It is a "culture of fear" that dominates the everyday life of individuals. In addition, the "Cuban diaspora" of the last fifty five years has fractured the Cuban family and dispersed Cubans across the world. In essence, long distances and the longing for family reunification who resided outside the island, could be considered contributing factors to the fact that only 22% of the individuals in our study indicated that they wanted to spend their free time with friends and relatives.

THE NATURE OF HUMAN BEINGS

This section of the survey was very important in understanding the value system of the recently arrived Cubans in South Florida. They were asked if there was a need to have laws in society. Slightly more than one-fourth of the persons in our sample (28%) believed that human beings are essentially evil. These individuals were more prone to experiencing distrust with regards to the motivations and intents of others. They were also prone to being hyper vigilant and paranoid, and to distrust not only the motivations of their peers, but also the motivations of their leaders or anyone in position of authority. These individuals tend to perceive authority as oppressive, persecutory and exploitative and may have difficulties adapting to a civil society, such as the one that exist in pluralistic societies, unless their trust is restored and their perceptions can change over time. A similar number of those individuals studied (30%), perceived that human beings are essentially good. This group will continue to place their hope and trust in others. A greater number of the respondents (42%) believed that human beings are neither good or bad, but that laws are necessary to maintain order. If we add the last two groups together, those who believe people are essentially good (30%) and those who are neutral (42%), we find that the great majority (72%) are not distrustful of others. These individuals have not given up on humanity. But see humans as responsive to their surrounding circumstances. As a consequence, these individuals are more likely to integrate successfully as part of a civil society where it is necessary to have a basic trust in authority and institutions that have been created for the common good. Not to oppress or abuse the citizens of their country. They are more likely to adapt to the rules and regulations of a civil society.

TRADITIONS VERSUS ADAPTATION: FAMILY VERSUS INDIVIDUAL

This part of the study addressed the current dilemma experienced in the daily lives of Cubans living on the island. The decision to abandon one's chosen profession for a position that will provide the individual the necessary means to survive is very important.

In this case we found that only a minority of those studied (15%) chose to consult with their superiors (paternalistic government authority), demonstrating either distrust, or a growing disengagement from the totalitarian authority that would have been expected in the earlier days of the revolution. We found that (42%), resolved their personal problems by consulting with someone of authority within their family more in keeping with the Pre-Revolutionary Cuban values and traditions. Individuals of Hispanic origin traditionally endow the head of the family, usually the father or grandfather and in some maternal families the mother or grandmother with the power and respect, which acknowledges that this person holds the highest position of authority (Bernal, 1982). It is important to note that even after fifty-five years of totalitarian control, a significant number of the individuals in the study still adhered to the tradition of placing the head of the family in the highest position of authority, a characteristic that is deeply ingrained in the Hispanic culture.

A slightly larger number of individuals (43%) decided to make their own decisions, demonstrating autonomy from both, the family hierarchy and the governmental authorities in their decision-making. Shiraev and Glad (1999) described how, in communist societies, obedience to government authority is strongly enforced and initiative and individualism are strongly discouraged. Both of them added that, individuals who have been raised under communism, when faced with any changes often become confuse about societal expectations that seem to run contrary to everything that they have learn until then. We found that the value system of the individuals in our study who chose their own self-determination (make their own decisions) was more congruent with the values of a capitalistic society with a free market economy, and therefore it could be assumed that this group will probably adapt quicker to living in the United States or other democratic societies. In these individuals alike many dissidents on the island, these particular values of initiative and self-determination run against the norms of acceptable behavior in a totalitarian society.

When analyzing our data further, we found a significant contradiction when comparing the responses to gender. Women were more likely to employ initiative and individual self-determination (49%) than men (39%), and less likely to consult with superiors (7%) than men (20%). However, men (41%) and women (44%) were comparably inclined to consult with the family authority. One possible explanation for this finding could be based on the fact that men in Cuba are more often the family's principal financial provider, and more likely to be present in the workplace, where obedience and conformity with the system are demanded. Women, on the other hand, are more likely to be connected with the daily procurement of taking care of the needs of the family, and thus may be able to use their creativity and work behind the curtain in order to provide for the family, even when this is done outside of the established government channels.

GOVERNMENT VERSUS FAMILY AND FRIENDS

This section of the study depicted a common scenario in the life of the average Cuban who might find themselves unable to support his or her family with their current government salary and are forced to consider other options outside the official channels to make ends meet.

We found that the minority of the respondents (12%) opted to ask the government for help, clearly indicating a diminishing trust and reliance on the paternalistic role of the Cuban government, as the main source of problem solving in the daily lives of Cubans. Another group (23%) opted to rely on family and friends for help, resorting to the Hispanic cultural and traditional modes of networking among family and friends (Bernal, 1982; Ruiz, 2001). A mode of relating to others that does not appear to have changed completely by the ideology of the revolution. However, the majority of those interviewed (65%) opted to find a second job (legally or illegally) demonstrating initiative, individualism, and self-reliance. This style of problem solving could be potentially problematic for the future under a democratic system if the individuals does not rely on institutions, organizations, and the rule of law. Yet at the same time, this individualistic spirit can be very positive in a free-market system.

INITIATIVE VERSUS BREAKING THE LAWS

In this section of our study we addressed the need to surviver vs. ethical dilemmas and the fear faced by Cubans who are subjected to a totalitarian system that forbids private enterprise, but at the same time is unable to adequately provide the basic needs for its citizens.

The scenario presented to the group being studied was " you discover that your son is dealing in the black market in order to survive. What will you do?" The majority of the respondents (89%) chose to do nothing assuming a passive stance, accepting with complacency the situation that was being expounded. Another small group (11%), chose to "tell him to stop" assuming an authoritarian moralistic stance, perhaps also taking into account the consequences involved if the individual is caught (fear). However, this option "closes the doors" and offers no other alternatives.

The great majority (70%) chose to tell him to "look for other alternatives." These respondents acknowledged the "need to obtain goods," possibly outside the official channels necessary for survival (Resolver). This respond could be interpreted in several ways. It can be interpreted to mean that the respondents are afraid of the "legal penalties the son would face," if he is caught (fear). It could also mean that the individual is facing an "ethical dilemma," forced to take a temporary action. Dealing in the black market becomes necessary for survival but which goes against the individual's moral make-up and therefore generates internal conflict. In either case scenario, it could be argued that the respondents in the study did not support the commonly held belief that the majority of modern day Cubans lack moral values. Society's moral character has been deformed by the communist ideology and the environment they lived in. These individuals were faced with serious ethical dilemmas and the situation of fear brought upon by the totalitarian system which placed them in an impossible situation (needing to break the rules in order to survive). We can also speculate that the individuals who chose to "look for other options" may be one that is experiencing internal conflict, having assumed a temporary solution to the problem of dealing with the black market, but who would not do so if offered other viable actions,.

The responses to the survey often times raised more questions than answers, and like many other similar studies and findings, they raise awareness of the need for more in depth research in order o better understand the value system of individuals who have lived for a long time under a totalitarian regime

POLITICAL OPINIONS

Finally, we included some scenarios and questions to the group being studied regarding their political opinions on the current situation in Cuba and a few "what if" situations for them to react and answer.

The first question had to do with the United States Economic Embargo on Cuba. Fifty-seven percent said they were against the economic embargo while 36% was in favorite. During our interviews we found that most of the respondents felt very strongly that normalizing relations with the United States was a key component in ameliorating the political, economic, and social changes of a transition in Cuba. In other words, improvement in US-Cuba relations was viewed as an important factor of alleviating the hardships on the island and perhaps helping to reduce the enormous challenge of rebuilding a Post-Castro Cuba.

The next important information we wanted to find out was how did Cubans on the island go about obtaining reliable information inside the Cuba. Seventy-one percent claimed they received most of their information by talking to people on the streets. While 14% said they received their information by talking to friends and relatives abroad. Today, you will find more cell phones and internet access in Cuba then ten years ago. However, both are expensive and not very reliable. Those individuals with cell phone are young and for most part live in urban areas. Miami Herald journalist Juan Tamayo, wrote an article (November 11, 2010) which said that there were over three-hundred illegal satellite connections on the island that Cubans use to watch television and get news. Cuba is still not up to par with the Middle East as far as the number of cell phones used by the population to communicate with each other during the "Arab Spring." The Cuban government still controls all the communication modes on the island and use it as a way of controlling the life of the people.

It is very important and worth noting that a big challenge for the government in the future will be how much the population will trust the information they hear each day from the state media. Talking to people on the street is an extremely unreliable source of news and information in a pluralistic society, a society that requires well informed and empowered citizens in a civil society. The high level of distrust that Cubans have on their state media can easily lead to political entrepreneurs using information to manipulate the political outcomes. A good example of using this techniques has been done in Venezuela. A respected and legitimate media, perceived as such by the public will be essential in a democratic state. However, this will take time to develop as well as accepting and trusting the media after so many years of distrust.

We also asked the group if Cuba's changed politically, whatt kind system of government would they prefer and what would they change first? Seventy-one percent said that they would like to see a democratic system of government. Twenty-four percent said that they did not know what type of government they would prefer. Forty-five percent of those surveyed said that they would change everything followed by 35% that would change the economy and 28% would change the laws of Cuba. There was a strong felling among the entire group that Cuba's problems were institutional. One can argue that this problem already existed prior to the Revolution of 1959. Democratic institutions are the mechanism by which policies are formulated and implemented. Therefore, one can argue that an institutional restructuring will be necessary if positive social, political, and policy outcomes are to be achieved by a new government. The difficult task will be changing the human values and attitudes of all Cubans to support such changes. This process can take an entire generation and the question remains, where do you start?

Cubans on the island are tired and overwhelmed by the dictatorship of the Castro's and the ideology of a system that has failed around the world. Escapism, high levels of frustration, and alienation are prevalent in the Cuban people today. This will be a challenge in terms of building a civil society that is engaged in running the country and developing new values and patterns of behavior.

The study also showed that 74% of Cubans living in exile would not go back to live other than to visit relatives and friends. Life for those that lived in Cuba for a long time has created such negative memories, that for those in exile the goal was to forget the past and start over. In addition, the results showed recent arrivals had a very positive view of the Cuban exile community and felt very welcomed. This can be attributed to the visits by Cuban-Americans to the island in recent years and their financial support for those left behind. In 2012 United States government data showed that approximately 476,000 Cuban-Americans visited the island.

TEN YEARS LATER

Between my first trip to Cuba in 2001 and my last trip in 2012 for Pope Benedict's visit, I continued my research on the values and attitudes of Cubans on the island and those recently arrived in South Florida. The second part of the study was divided into two groups; (1) Those individuals that originally participated in the study conducted in 2002 and now lived in South Florida. Many members of this group since arriving had gone back to Cuba to visit relatives and friends. and (2) Those individuals that were interviewed individually and in groups of five during my trip to Cuba.

The same methodology was used for both groups. However, for the study in 2012, a survey was not used. Instead open-ended questions were used for the purpose of getting the individuals to speak freely on each topic. The data collected from this group was then compared with the data collected from the first group of 2002.

FIRST GROUP OF 2002

After the original meetings and interviews with this group of participants, I was able to contact approximately half of them and follow-up after their first year in the United States and then I followed-up again after ten years. Many of them had relocated to other parts of the United States where they had other family members or friends. One of the participants had returned to live in Cuba. It is important to remember that all of these participants were born in Cuba after the Cuban Revolution of 1959 and had left the island until arriving in the United States.

For those individuals that arrived with a relative or friend and had relatives and friends that lived in South Florida or other parts of the United States, their adjustment to the regular routines of daily life was a little better than those that came alone and had no support system. After spending several weeks settling in a new environment, their first task was to find a place to live and a job. Most in this group were provided assistance by the various social agencies in the area. One observation made by many of the respondents was how much food was available and the free access that they had to information all over the world including inside Cuba. This included the names of dissidents and opposition leaders who they had never heard before. For example, a twenty-three year old male told me when I asked him what he had done his first week in Miami, "I spent as much time possible on my aunt's computer looking for news and reading stories around the world." He went on to ask me, " what happened to Yugoslavia?" There were many other questions from other participants similar to this two. This was a clear sign of how effective the Cuban government has been in controlling information from its citizens.

Many in the group still wanted to talk about their struggles in Cuba. The lack of food, poor housing, lack of jobs, poor transportation which makes for a difficult way of living each day. After living for some time outside Cuba, many were still struggling emotionally and found it difficult in getting a good job but still preferred to be living in the United States. For those individuals who had no relatives or friends when they arrived in South Florida it had been more difficult to adjust. After all this time many still depended on social agencies and organizations for basic support hoping that as the years continue to pass it would get better. As a young female told me, "at least there is hope for the future. We had none in Cuba."

As indicated before, most of these individuals were born after the start of the Cuban Revolution. They grew up being indoctrinated from their early years in an ideology that put the state's needs ahead of their personal needs. They lived in a "culture of fear" each day afraid of speaking out against things they felt were wrong with the totalitarian system of government. They lived in an environment that shaped their value system and personal behavior. As a man in his early thirties told me, " I woke up each morning knowing that I had to steal and cheat to provide for my family. I had no choice. As timed passed it became part of my daily routine. It became an acceptable moral value that I had no control over it."

As glad as they were living in the United States, many in the group suffered during the first year from some form of depression or psychological trauma. Many missed Cuba, their relatives and friends. They became somewhat nostalgic for the way things worked in Cuba. This was very similar to those individuals in Central and Eastern Europe during their transition. This was not because things were better in Cuba. They had become accustomed how to live within the guidelines set by the government. Many found it difficult living in a free society. They had no idea how to participate in a civil society or more important they lacked civic skills. For those who had now been in the United States for over ten years, 65% were still not US citizens and most had not joined any civic group or organization. Shortly after I completed this follow-up study, a young man in his mid-twenties informed me that he was returning to live in Cuba because he did not know what to do with all these new acquired freedoms.

About one-third of the individuals that were married when they arrived to the United States were now divorced. Most blamed it on the stress and anxieties of coping in a new environment. One they were not used to it. One of the original members of our research team, Dr. Hector Matos (Psychiatrist) told me that on a regular basis he counseled recently arrived Cubans suffering from many psychological disorders such as anxieties, symptoms of chronic low mood, lack of interest, and sleep disorders recurring nightmares, poor concentration and generally impaired functions. This was mainly due to their past lives in Cuba and now trying to adapt to a new system. The older the individual was, the more problems they had adjusting. Another member of our team of researchers, Dr. Eugenio Rothe (Psychiatrist) told me that he counseled many children who had terrible problems adapting to their new schools and new friends. For them the education no longer emphasized any particular ideology and they were free to speak in class. Many told Dr. Rothe that they no longer had to worry about whether they were going to eat each day or not. According to Dr. Rothe, one particular boy exhibited a great deal of fear towards people in uniform, particularly policemen. This is an example of the destruction of trust between individuals created by the ideology he had been taught in Cuba. It leads to a wider cooperation and collaborative behavior between individuals.

To understand the feeling and behaviors of these individuals, we must realize that many of the policies of a totalitarian state like Cuba have the potential of causing severe psychological distress even after the person leaves the country. In order to legitimize its own existence the state (Cuba) constantly creates internal and external conflict against real and imaginary enemies such as the fear of an invasion from the United States or the Cuban-American community in South Florida returning one day to Cuba and claiming all their properties and leaving people homeless and out of work. These observations leads one to believe that mental health issues in a Post-Castro Cuba will be an important priority for a future government to deal with.

Most people that have left Cuba have done so because they do not support the government and they are seeking a better future. The individuals that were originally interviewed for the 2002 study mostly agreed they left Cuba because there was no future and economically it was impossible to live under those conditions. However, we still found that some had some positive views towards the Cuban government and its leaders.

A year later, the same group was less positive about their futures in exile which is a very similar characteristic found in many post-totalitarian states. In general, the group spoke about how difficult it had been to assimilate to a new society in the United States. Many of their original plans for the future like getting good job, advancing their education, buying a car, etc. had to be postponed. Even though most of the things they lacked in Cuba were available in their new community, they were expensive and out of their reach. As an older woman told me during an interview, " In Cuba the state provided for everything. It was not much but we made ends meet." After the first year in exile, some of the participants had started to have doubts about coming to the United States. For many the solution was to go back to Cuba to visit relatives and friends. As an older man explained to me, "I live in two worlds, in Miami and in Cuba. I'm afraid that this is my future, providing for myself in exile and providing for my family back in Cuba." In 2012 it was estimated that approximately 476,000 Cuban had traveled back to the island for a visit taking back money and goods and other essentials for their families and friends.

One of the last interviews I conducted was with a couple that came together and got married shortly after they arrived in Miami. They told me that they were uncertain about their futures. But one thing they knew for sure was that they would never set foot in Cuba again. They also believed that it would be a long time before Cuba would become a democratic state. The people are not prepared to sustain such a system.

2012 TRIP TO CUBA

Early in 2012 Miami's Catholic Archbishop Thomas Wenski invited me to go on a pilgrimage to Cuba for Pope Benedict's visit in March of 2012. The Archbishop wanted me to see all the good work the church had been doing throughout the island. It had almost been eleven years since my trip to Cuba on 2001. I agreed to go along as long as the Cuban government would let me enter Cuba. In 2001, the Cuban government protested to the United States Department of State my presence on the island. This time a friend who used to be a Cuban intelligence officer negotiated my entry permission (Visa) with the Cuban Foreign Ministry.

After much preparation and anticipation the day came. The short trip to out first stop Santiago de Cuba was not long. When we landed, our plane was surrounded by Cuban military for security reasons. Pope Benedict was to celebrate the first mass on the plaza late that afternoon and afterwards we would fly to Havana for the second mass the following day. My goal during my visit to Cuba was to meet and interview as many young Cubans as possible using the same methodology and techniques that were used in the original study in 2001. I would then compare both data sets to see if the values and attitudes of Cubans had changed and how.

The island of Cuba has a population of approximately 11.2 million people of which about 65% are Afro-Cubans. In Santiago de Cuba located on the eastern part of the island, most of the population is Afro-Cuban (85%) so all the individuals I met and interviewed were

Afro-Cubans. Very different from the participants of 2001 who were all white. In Havana the population is more mixed (60% Afro-Cuban and 40% white). This would give me the opportunity to study a group (Afro-Cubans) whose opinions had not been asked often. In Havana I had the opportunity to meet and interview members of both races. I should mention that I had the opportunity to interview as many men as women.

The first interviews conducted in Santiago de Cuba were done both individually and in small groups. All the participants had university degrees in professional fields that were difficult to find jobs in. All of them worked in the tourist industry or were unemployed. They spoke good English they had learned in school and was required to work in the tourist industry in Cuba. All the participants were very forthcoming with their stories. In Havana, it was very easy to find young people to talk to. They were everywhere and willing to sit down and have a cup of Cuban coffee. All of them had university degrees. In both cities these young people described how they had grown up learning and believing in a Marxist ideology that they no longer supported. They had very little interest for politics. They wanted a better future than what the Cuban government could offer them. For the Afro-Cubans, the Cuban Revolution had promised them a better life and for most part it had failed to deliver. They were very frustrated with the progress they had made in fifty years. It was cleared that they lacked information. Less than 10% of both groups had access to the internet or even owned a computer. Less than 5% own a cell phone. Most claimed that the information they received via television and radio was government propaganda and could not be trusted. Occasionally they would watch old movies that had been brought from Miami. A very important observation was the fact that all participants wanted to know about the United States and the

Cuban-American community in South Florida. They exhibited no ill well towards the Cubans in exile.

I asked both groups if they had heard of Yoani Sanchez, Oswaldo Paya or other Cuban dissidents on the island and only 15% had. It was clear how effective the Cuban government has been in controlling the information.

The youngsters I interviewed were fairly well adjusted. However, they showed a high degree of frustration with the Cuban government economic reforms and how long they were taking to implement them. Most of the participants had come to the realization that the Cuban leadership was only interested in keeping political power. They spoke about their parents and grandparents dissolution with the Cuban Revolution. Some of the participants had suffered from some type of psychological disorder in the last five years. Many in the group had turned to music as a way of expressing their frustration through the lyrics of the songs. Others wanted to leave the country but were worry about leaving their families and friends behind. Many claimed that they were able survive each day by creating a very close group of friends and relatives that they could trust and count on for moral support. However, others still feared the negative consequences if they spoke openly against the government.

Finally, I came to the conclusion that most of these youngsters wanted to leave Cuba under any circumstances. When I asked if a democratic system of government would replace the totalitarian regime of the Castro brothers and most said yes, but that it would take a very long time to convince the people that this type of "change" in the long run would benefit all.

On January 1, 2014, Raul Castro spoke in Santiago de Cuba to mark the 55th anniversary of the Cuban Revolution and he said, " the challenge is growing each day, there is a permanent campaign of subversion, specially aimed at our youth. We are perceiving attempts to subtly introduce platforms for neoliberal and capitalist ideas that favor individualism, egoism, and mercantilism. The insidious campaign is designed to dismantle Cuba's socialism from the inside by disseminating ideas that deny the vitality of Marxist-Leninist concepts and those of Cuban Independence." (32)

During this last trip to Cuba I found that it is the very ideas Raul Castro warned young people about that they want. The revolution's ideology is no longer a reality. I also left the island with a better understanding that a transition to democracy will require time and a psychological transformation of those on the island and tolerance from those in exile.

CHAPTER THREE

CHALLENGES IN DEVELOPING
A CIVIL SOCIETY IN CUBA

Although Cuban political culture since the Republic (1902-1959) has exhibited a pro-democratic interest, a host of attitudes, affective tendencies, and political behaviors have most of the time corroded civic democratic life. According to Professor Damian Fernandez, the results created weak governments, weak leaders, weak institutions, and a few dictators. The primary normative foundation for Cuban incivility. (33).

Cubans today are apathetic and lack confidence in political institutions. The young have opted out of the system. The economy offers few rewards for those who follow the law, so lawlessness is rampant. Cubans have had to resort to the illegal informal sector (Resolver) to survive and are consequently socialized to break the law. The duplicitous morality many have opted espouses one set of criteria in public and a different one in private. Stealing from the state is not perceived as taking something that is not yours. At times, Cubans seem to want to be free from politics rather than agents of it, while holding the same high expectations of what the state should provide.

Today, civil society is mostly controlled by the government and can hardly be considered civil. Repression and intolerance continue as ways of dealing with political dissidents and opponents of the regime. Autonomous associations and organizations have very little space to operate and have any impact in the daily life of Cubans. The Cuban people have resorted to informal networks to satisfy both material and non-material needs, reinforcing a penchant for anti-institutionalism.

Any post-totalitarian government will have to deal with these social-cultural values and behaviors. This does not mean that most Cubans do not yearn for democratic participation. They do! But will their cultural proclivities, political, cultural, and social norms sustain or undermine a civic culture and democratic future?

Do the current values and behaviors of the Cuban people support or subvert a future democratic system of government? After fifty-five years of a totalitarian system, one can assume that the current Cuban political culture tends to undermine democratic life, the question we should be asking ourselves is, how can we transform the people's values and attitudes to support a democratic form of government? This is the real challenge that future leaders will face. Neither the historical record of fostering change in values nor the experiences of democratic culture in Cuba is very promising under the existing social, economic, and political environment.

The quest for democracy in Cuba is not new. Its roots are as old as the attempts to generate effective, legitimate, and representative institutions upon the birth of the Republic in 1902. The aspirations ran through Catholic priest, Father Felix Varela to Jose Marti, the founding father of the nation and it continued through scores of intellectuals and politicians of the early republic. For instance, the fight against corruption motivated thousands of Cubans in the 1950"s to support the Cuban Revolution.

Sine 1959, the Cuban government has expressed attitudes and values as part of their Marxist ideology that repels democratic ideals. Cuban culture and the values it carries appeared resilient, although not susceptible to change. In the case of the country's political system, authoritarian and civil norms have been institutionalized in formal structures and legislation since 1959. Given that this is the case, then how are civic values to be fostered, promoted, institutionalized and sustained to facilitate democratic principles in a post-transition? The following shows a sample of this process.

CHANGE PROCESS

Totalitarian Control
Transition Movement
Transformation of Human Values and Attitudes
Development of a Civil Society
Democratic Institutions Established
Preservation and Maintenance of the New Democratic System

This process can take time and there is no model in any other part of the world that could apply to Cuba one-hundred percent. Different societies in different political systems rest on divergent set of values. Successful democracies rest not only on effective and legitimate institutions and good leadership, but also on citizens who espouse a pro-democratic spirit. Without deciding which of the three dimensions of democracy is most important, one can conclude that values and political culture contribute to the making or the unmaking of social capital, civility, and democracy. What is clear, though, is that some values promote democracy more effectively than others. Likewise, institutions support or fail to support civic democratic culture. The issue of engineering values is an attempt to advance democratic culture, is one of the most daunting social issues for scholars and policy makers to understand. Changing institutions is easier than altering human behavior and personal aspirations.

In my opinion, Cuban culture has some traditions of democratic thought and ideals throughout its history. However, we also find less than pro-democratic patterns that have corroded civic democratic practices. Values such as social solidarity, equity and state responsibility for the economic needs of the less fortunate predate 1959, although socialism underscored them. In fact, the social democratic aspect of Cuban political culture attained its maximum expression in the republic in the form of the constitution of 1940 that legislated a strong welfare state within the context of democracy. Unfortunately, the civic life of the republic was tarnished by corruption and finally a military coup.

I further argue that judging from the sources that shaped Cuba's political culture, Cuban society has not advocated in practice the Anglo-American liberal variant of democracy. The norms and the networks of social capital in Cuba have gone against the ideal notions of democracy, liberal economics, and civil society. Acknowledging the particularity of Cuban political culture, the difficulty in changing it, and the possibility of the rise of an uncivil society in a post-communist transition should serve to adjust our expectations in the future. There are many examples around the world.

The question regarding which values promote democracy has a counterpoint; which institutions promote democratic values? To do so, formal institutions should be based on the rule of law. They ought to respect the separation of powers within the government as well. They should guarantee property rights, the right to organize competitive political parties, and free and fair elections, and the right to create civil associations. Formal institutions should also promote a market economy. A key factor in this entire process is the promotion of democratic norms and values throughout the population at all ages by using the education system. Citizen participation is vital and civic values are desirable. Only by promoting both can it prevent the possibility of the resurgence of an uncivil society, one based on intolerance for contending political control.

VALUES AND DEMOCRACY

Values expressed in political culture define our personal and collective interests. Societies nationalistic values define what is desirable. They bind people together and provide the basis for social identity. Analyzing the values of a society provides a lens through which to interpret world views, its behavior and ideals, its sense of good and evil, and its evaluations of the material. Some basic values relate to the material needs that guarantee the continuation of life. Others conform the rights, duties and moral principles of the collectivity; they bring together the basis for the good life. In practice, values constitute the basis for public policies and politics (Carrow et al. 1998). Values shift as a result of: (1) Low term processes of structural change, such as an economic shift, (2) Generational foundational experiences such as the civil rights movements in the United States; (3) Institutional restructuring; (4) Education; and (5) Change in family socialization during the early stages of personality formation (34).

Major value shifts tend to take time. However, we must keep in mind that values can shift in either direction, towards or away from democratic norms. Therefore, democratic transitions are the result of several inter-related factors in tandem, from the decision of leaders to institutional engineering, not to mention the impact of economics. Since 1990, a number of countries that have exhibited a cultural propensity to both attract and repel democracy have been relatively successful in instituting systems of multiple political parties in free and fair elections as well as establishing a vibrant civil society and respect for human rights. Cuba does not have to be the exception.

The political culture of a country is just one dimension that helps shape political outcomes. While no particular future is guaranteed, the cultural tendency of Cubans to construe politics as a moral crusade for absolute ends is very much alive. This is what many scholars call "The Politics of Passion" while to behave in everyday life in ways in which justify the means, even if breaking the rule of law is required to satisfy personal needs is referred to as "The Politics of Affection."

CHALLENGES IN CREATING CIVIC VALUES IN A TRANSITION

The challenges confronting the construction of civic values are immense. In the case of Cuba, accepting the fact that "change" will be better than the current political system will be difficult. The exploitation by the current government of national symbols and myths, such as the founding father of the nation Jose Marti, might have discredited them in the minds of the younger generation who will play a crucial role in the future of Cuba. Rescuing these values as a rallying point will not be an easy process. The exhaustion people have with politics, political propaganda, and the lack of trust in them will make getting the attention of the population even harder. To complicate matters, value priorities tend to be place on the needs that are in short supply (Inglehart 1977) (31), which in the context of economic scarcity translates into maternal values of economic security being overvalued as compared to post-maternal ones. Key economic sectors will be the stronghold of communist elites and out of reach for the state as for the average citizen. Similar to what we find in Russia today under Vladimir Putin.

In Cuba, the experience of a totalitarian government both exacerbates and facilitates the challenge of promoting a civic culture. This is compounded by some of the negative patterns accentuated in the last fifty-five years. The individuals dependence on the state, the everyday illegal patterns of behavior, corruption, and the rejection of politics due to over-socialization have been aggravated during the revolution. This behavior has led to a reluctance by the citizens to participate in politics,

The tradition of democracy in its civil and social dimensions must be rescued and restored in a post-Castro Cuba to counter the tendency towards incivility, illegality, corruption, and authoritarianism. The "everything goes" mentality widespread in sectors of the population must be balanced with the concern for the common good.

CUBAN POLITICAL CULTURE AND VALUES

Cuban values and political culture are a combination of liberal-modern and informal traditions. Together, these paradigms have promoted and subverted democratic practice. The conflict between the ideal aspiration for democracy and the real corruption of that project in the past has facilitated the construction of politics as a concept for absolute ends or the "Politics of Passion." (36) While at the same time aspiring for a collective good, Cubans have acted in ways that have undermined the goal of pursuing "Socialism" or the "Politics of Affection," (37) which breaks the law for self-serving reasons. Both the politics of passion and affection have defined the character of politics in Cuba and in exile, particularly found among the recent arrivals. The politics of passion comes from the moral judgements regarding the cap between what is and what ought to be in the political and social sphere. The politics of affection are both a product and producer of the pervasive informality found in the social sphere, and it reflects the weakness of formal institutions addressing the basic needs of the people.

The adoption of Marxism as the official ideology of Cuba in 1961, two years after the triumph of the revolution, did not represent as big a cultural watershed as initially expected by the leadership. In Cuba the communist ideology was able to put aside a long-standing aspiration for modernization, social equality, order, and sovereignty similar to the United States and on the romanticism of Cuba political culture since the colonial era, later fostered by Jose Marti. Marxism offered a material and moral utopia for the community. The emphasis on collective harmony and regulation in society contradicts modern democratic notions of self-interest and the conflicting nature of social relations and neglects the informal conduct of individualism in their daily life, "Lo Informal"(38). "Lo Informal" is closer to a pattern of behavior, with its own logic, norms, vocabulary, and emotional infrastructure, than an explicitly intellectual framework ("A la Cubana"). Informality undermines the tenets of rationality. Cuba reproduced 'Lo Informal" as a way of dealing with, if not circumventing, the needs of self, the family and community, This practice is still very common in the Cuban exile community as well.

The values of informality plays a significant role of person to person contact, and the bond of affection among family members and friends above the impersonal norms of the government. Informality depends on the possibility of bending the rules and bypassing legal norms because "we are special." Its capacity to rationalize each and every action on the basis that what is most important is to satisfy one's own needs and those of one's loved ones seems infinite. Precisely because of its immense capacity to justify what could be considered self-serving, the normative foundation of informal behavior usually suffers from civic myopia; it fails to see what is beyond the networks of affection and disregards in the process the significance of institutions for the common good. Although being informal is not usually a positive trait in Cuban society, there is a benign appreciation for it.

"Lo informal" is not unrelated to the "Choteo" (mockery). According to Professor Damian Fernandez, "mockery is a peculiar Cuban brand of humor that is part of the informal norms. Its comic peculiarity is that it targets authority, with the purpose of undermining hierarchy, order, and regulations. Mockery de-authorizes authority by debunking it and it constitutes a form of rebellion. It is undisciplined and not very serious. It reflects contempt for and cynicism about higher-ups and the institutions of society." (39)

Importantly at the grassroots it has a paradoxical impact on governance. While it establishes trust and collaboration among small groups of individuals and allows for the manifestation of divergent passions, interests, and identities, it undermines larger associations whose membership is not limited to personal contact. Some of the affective aspects and networks of the informal norms are important to the foundation of a civil society. The seeds of civic virtue and civic associations are to be found in a similar emotional infrastructure of solidarity and trust. The challenge is how to translate the norms of "Lo Informal" into ones that help to bind individuals into larger organizations and the community.

Informal practices are functional for those engaged in them as well as for the government. On a personal level, they provide satisfaction of needs. It is also a way of getting around the bureaucracy of everyday. At the same time, participation in "Lo informal" socializes individuals in a culture of illegality. It accustoms them to break the law and thus undermines the tenets of the regime and creates incivility. The more you do it, the more it becomes a regular pattern of behavior that becomes an acceptable value. The concept to "resolver" in Cuba today is a perfect example.

Cuban politics have been characterized by both a movement for moral ends for the nation and a campaign for personal gratification. Politics have represented a crusade to save the nation. While society in general aspired to a higher level of moral political order, in their daily practice, social actors have undermined their lofty collective aspirations through their resort to informality and anti-institutionalism. The result is a loss of faith in the big projects of the modern state and results in a national masochistic act or event.

The irony is that the Cuban people, although disenchanted with their lives and government, they have not totally abandoned their aspirations for a new and improved system of government. They continue to act in everyday life in ways that are detrimental to the normative models they wish for. In the long run, Cuban political culture will tend to have a contradictory impact on political transition and democratization. The politics of passion will exert their multiple influences on governance and social life in ways that are not narrowly liberal, if and when democracy is established in Cuba.

SOCIAL CAPITAL IN CUBA

Social capital can be considered the norms and networks of society that can contribute to civic mindedness, which in turn has positive repercussions on economic productivity and governmental performance. Not all societies seem to be endowed with the same social capital. As a source of social capital, Cuban informality and its networks based on exclusionary and particularistic criteria, such as affection, kinship, and friendship, could pose challenges in forming a vibrant civil society in Cuba in the future. Though the networks of 'Lo informal" will help establish economic enterprises as friends and family form organizations in a more open political system, the Cuban variant of social capital could continue to bypass the rule of law and subvert the state. While the social capital of "Lo informal" has generated trust and collaboration, it has done so in relatively small groups. The networks of "Lo informal" will continue to favor personal connections and will tend to justify any and all actions in so far as they satisfy personal desires. Combined with the morally charged issues, challenges, and uncertainties that any transition is likely to carry, the logic of the ends justify the means that is typical of Cuban culture probably will be reproduced, as a consequence of setting the foundation for an uncivil society.

SOCIAL POLITICAL VALUES

At a different scale of analysis, the features of Cuban political values, attitudes, and behavior, particularly under communism include: (1) Social responsibility of the state, which favors a welfare policy for the less fortunate to guarantee a minimum standard of well being as well as equity. Reliance on the state has been changing since the 1990's. With the fall of the Soviet Union that created an economic crisis (Special Period) Cubans have restored more to self-help initiatives and grass-root responses to the problems they face each day as the state and local governments no longer respond to the regular needs of the population. (2) Nationalism in two versions, reformist and radical, which can coexists with a rejection of patriotic symbols. (3) A proclivity toward anti-institutionalism and personalism. (4) A tendency toward spontaneity and order. (5) The penchant towards "El Choteo" (mockery). (6) De-socialization coexisting with socialization contributes to pervasive illegality, breaking the official norms of conduct. (7) Anti-work attitudes due to the lack of material incentives for work. (8) Pessimism towards the future. (9) Lack of basic social trust due to the fear generated by coercive government threats. (10) Breakdown of family structure, and (11) Leave Cuba as the only option.

IMPACT OF CUBAN VALUES ON GOVERNABILITY

The combination of previously mentioned values, and behavioral patterns will challenge any type of government in a post-Castro transition. They will impact the quality and style of democracy that Cuba develops as well as the political and civil society that will emerge post-transition, tending to imprint the general social fabric with possible incivility. Taken within the context of insecurity, uncertainty, and material deprivation that is likely during transition, governance could be difficult. The economy of scarcity typical of Cuban socialism, likely to continue during and immediately following a transition, does not provide for the most fertile ground for civic values to prosper. A number of these negative attitudes can be changed by altering the education system and providing real incentives for work and by providing opportunities for political engagement at all levels in which political and civic participation is authentic.

The Cuban people do have some values and behavior attitudes that are amenable to the creation of an energetic civil society. In conjunction with a relatively high level of education and an entrepreneur spirit. Cuban society has a partial foundation for "change" that can lead to a free and democratic state. However, it will take time to evolve and sustain a new civil society in Cuba.

NONDEMOCRATIC CONTINUITY

Political strategies regarding political regimes like the one in Cuba can be presented in a continuum from low to high degree of change of the authoritarian rule the actors tend to introduce. Many scholars and "Cuba Watchers" expected that once Fidel Castro was out of the picture, the entire system would collapsed. It has been eight years since Fidel transfer power to his younger brother Raul and so far the system has survived.

Nondemocratic continuity represents a zero degree of change. So far all the reforms introduced and implemented by Raul Castro show a lack of giving up political control and allowing for the development of an organized civil society inside Cuba. In comparison to the Gorbachev strategy in the old Soviet Union which called for moderate political and social reforms in order to create intermediate outcomes between dictatorship and democracy.

In some cases, an intermediate strategy can promote a liberalization of the dictatorship, which can induce the formation of new reformist and opposition actors such as Lech Walesa in Poland which pushed further more changes in the process of democratization and the creation of a vibrant opposition party (Solidarity) which led to a strong civil society movement. This is not the case in Cuba.

However, some incumbent rulers can conceive moderate and intermediate reforms as a safety net for themselves and a way to create relatively stable situation away from the dictatorship but short of democracy. The idea of a continuum of political regimes is based on a minimalist definition of democratic regimes. Democracy can be defined simply as the appointment of leaders by voting which is exactly the system currently in place in Cuba. A democratic regime is based on a broad suffrage not excluding any significant social group, makes all relevant offices and decisions accountable, and develops political freedom and political party competition. In contrast to the concentration of power in the hands of an absolute single winner in non-democratic regimes. A high degree of democracy tends to produce multiple winners on different issues, power sharing between different parties, or frequent alternation of winners.

Different degrees of democracy correspond to different answers to the question of who votes, on what issues, and how. The outcomes are pre-determined and highly controlled such as the Cuban National Assembly, which is more of a ratifying body than a legislative body on public policy issues. Therefore, in order to build a workable model, three basic strategies can be identify in the face of an authoritarian regime according to Professor Josep Colomer. (40) These are: (1) Continuity of the non-democratic regime. In the case of communist regimes, it includes the maintenance of authoritarian institutions and state control of the economy. (2) Intermediate reforms leading to a limited democracy or a mixed economy. Those who favor this strategy may want to enlarge the inclusiveness of the authoritarian regime, allowing in particular a certain degree of freedom of speech and multiparty elections, perhaps to make it more stable. Regarding the economy in communist regimes, an intermediate reform strategy may involve some reduction of state control and the introduction of limited market relations in order to improve the efficiency of the system. However, it also includes restrictions on the activity of social groups, the maintenance of certain basic political institutions out of the electoral competition. In the case of Cuba controlled by the communist party, and finally state ownership of significant parts of the economy (Grupo Gaesa). Finally, (3) Democratic rupture with the legal and institutional framework of the authoritarian regime. This includes the initiation of a constituent process for the establishment of democracy and in transition from communist regimes.

CONCLUSION

Historically, a regime's response to civic activism can indeed prolong or shorten a struggle, but rarely does it manage to stamp resistance out entirely. Just recently we witnessed a complete turn around in Egypt's "Arab Spring." Thousands of Egyptians returned to iconic Tahrir Square to mark the third anniversary of the 2011 uprising that led to the overthrow of long time leader Hosni Mubarak and to what many people thought then was the promise of political reform. While the square at times resembled the breathtaking scenes of 2011, when hundreds of thousands Egyptians crammed every available space for eighteen days in a call for "change", now the square was instead a testimony to how much Egyptians rejected the same "change" they demanded at the same site in 2011.

Alexis de Tocqueville compared political and social institutions of a society to rivers that flow underground only to reemerge later at a different place. This is the perfect metaphor for building a civil society movement across the entire island of Cuba. If the offenses to dignity that have been committed by the Cuban regime are not challenged by the people, then no one else is to blame for the continuation of the violation of human rights and lack of freedom and liberty that could lead one day to a true democracy.

CHAPTER FOUR

THE ROLE OF EDUCATION IN CREATING CIVIL SOCIETY

During any transition it will take some time for the new changes introduced by a new government to rearrange themselves in patterns that will seem appropriate to a changing environment. Of the institutions central to the perpetuation of Cuba's communist regime, education was the most jealously guarded because it represented the process of ideological transfer, without which the state had no claim on its citizenry.

Communist societies such as Cuba consider "ideas" weapons in the class struggle. They stress the function of education in facilitating political indoctrination of the population and value education as a way to foster social equality. Without question, the long years of Soviet domination and central planning have inhibited the restructuring of the education system in former Soviet countries and Cuba will not be an exception.

The phrase "Nations in Transition" is usually referred to former communist countries (Birzea, 1994)(41). However, the concept of educational transition is equally applicable to other countries that have experienced a transformation in their education system following a political transition from an authoritarian regime to a democratic type of government.

In order to understand the process of education transition, it is necessary to first establish exactly what it means. The concept of education transition is defined in broad terms with the help of the model depicted below. This model is offered as a tool to assist in the description and explanation of the education transition process that have occurred following recent political transitions from authoritarian rule to a democratic government.

This model was created by Oxford Studies in Comparative Education, a small group of research scholars in Oxford, England in 1995. The group's intention was to create a model that could undergo considerable modification according to the needs of each country which is a very important concept when comparing historical, cultural, and environmental factors of each nation's experiences.

The initial stage of the model intends to contrast certain conditions of education systems as they move from authoritarianism to democracy. This contrast led the Oxford Group to develop a list of descriptors and their opposites as reflected in the table below: (42)

AUTHORITARIAN CONTROL		DEMOCRATIC GOVERNMENT
CERTAINTY	*VS*	*UNCERTAINTY*
UNIFORMITY	*VS*	*DIVERSITY*
CONFORMITY	*VS*	*INDIVIDUALITY*
CONTROL	*VS*	*AUTONOMY*
RIGIDITY	*VS*	*FLEXIBILITY*
STABILITY	*VS*	*INSTABILITY*
PREDICTABILITY	*VS*	*UNPREDICTABILITY*
DOGMA	*VS*	*PLURALISM*
CENTRALIZATION	*VS*	*DECENTRALIZATION*
CENSORSHIP	*VS*	*FREEDOM OF SPEECH*
NATIONALIZATION	*VS*	*PRIVATIZATION*

The term "transition" is used in common discourse to refer to changes in such areas as age, occupation, and social status. The tendency to equate changes and transition this way and to view life as "but a constant succession of changes in transition." (Birzea, 1994) have prompted certain scholars to define transition as "a permanent state of discontinuity in personal and communal life." (Adams and Birzea, 1994) (43) However, the concept of transition which I address in this book is a far more complex phenomenon. It cannot simply be equated with change that is defined as no more than a variation, an alteration, or the substitution of one thing or another.

Similarly, the standard use of the word "reform" fails to capture the essence of the transition processes addressed later in the book, and thus the use of "change" and "reform" interchangeably with "transition" in this context would distort the essence of political, social, and economic transformations that have occurred in many of the former Soviet Countries since 1989 or the "'Arab Spring" of 2010. The educational transition processes in these countries following the collapse of the incumbent totalitarian regimes transpired not because of a simple change in government, but because of the wholesale transformation or transition of the prevailing political system.

THE CASE OF CUBA

As we have learned from some of the transitions around the world, it is not easy to demolish fifty-five years of totalitarian control by the Castro's without addressing the issue of "value reconstruction." The civil society that must emerge in Cuba has to establish new social norms as it breaks down an ideological system that has had total social control of its citizens and is the only thing that they have experienced.

Cuba is an excellent case study of a political system that has exercised effective government social control over ideology and political culture and has maintained a centralized planned society for a long period of time. The prevailing system has successfully reduced conceptual sophistication about ideologies of resistance by emphasizing the importance of "collective well being of the state and not the individual" (Aguirre, 2002) (44). Additionally, the system has broken down the ability of individuals to claim ownership of central historical experiences, beliefs, values, and myths that a new education system will have to restore during a transition to democracy.

Any totalitarian government that has been in power as long as that of Cuba's, has had the opportunity to create institutions, collective memories, and facts or explanations of how the world operates as part of a cogent national cultural policy. Countries such as Cuba have had total control of the education system and have used it as a vehicle to indoctrinate children from an early age at schools through its curriculum and symbols. The system has also controlled mass media by creating a monopoly on the information and interpretations Cubans use everyday to make sense of their social world. In other words, the Cuban regime provides the explanations that become the "officially imagined world" that gives the government political legitimacy (Berger, 1990) (45). This type of control legitimizes the ideology of the government and creates a system of symbols and meanings that employ rhetorical devices to "establish and sustain relations of domination" (Thompson, 1990) (46) that bring about political stability.

The ability of Cuba's government social control systems to neutralize social movement organizations has pushed dissidence and the development of civil society into less organized and less institutionalized forms, such as mass behavior rather than individual patterns of behavior.

It will be up to the new education system to attempt to create and sustain a system of social change that will bring about the development of a new civil society and a concept of the individual. However, the implementation of these new norms and values as discussed earlier in the book will have to be established slowly and with a great deal of flexibility for them to work. Otherwise, Cuba will replicate what has occurred in some of the post-communist states, where the new system confuses citizens who have subsequently become nostalgic for the old ways. Not because they were better, but because they knew how to behave within those restrictions. As mentioned earlier, "change" is not only difficult but it also has different meaning according to the age group, cultural experiences, and environmental factors. (47)

TEACHING CIVIC EDUCATION FOR A DEMOCRATIC TRANSITION

The ideas of liberty, democracy, and constitutionalism have risen in the world as the bastions of totalitarian communism have continued to collapse. Meanwhile, the newly empowered citizens of post-communist countries have tried to build democratic foundations for their evolving nations. These countries have understood that a new curriculum for their schools are as important as new constitutions for their governments. Among other educational goals, they have recognized that schools must teach young citizens the theory and practices of constitutional democracy if they are to develop and sustain free societies and free governments.

An effective curriculum for teaching constitutional democracy must address civic knowledge, civic skills, civic virtues, and the role of the teacher. Educators of different countries may treat these themes differently according to their culture and specific needs, but certain themes are universal.

CIVIC KNOWLEDGE

The first objective of civic education is to teach the most basic civic idea, what a constitutional democracy is and what is not. If students are to be prepared to act as citizens of a democracy, they must know how to distinguish this type of government from other types. The label constitutional Democracy, has often been employed by regimes with showcase constitutions that proclaim popular governments and individual rights but have meant little or nothing to the regime's victims of tyranny. The people's democracies of former communist countries are examples of the bogus use of political labels.

Through civic education in schools, students should develop defensible criteria by which to think critically and to evaluate the extent to which their government and other governments of the world do or do not function authentically as constitutional democracies. The curriculum must include key concepts necessary to an understanding of constitutional democracy. These are: (1) Rule of law, (2) Limited government, (3) Representative government, (4) Individual rights, (5) Popular sovereignty, (6) Political participation, and (7) Civil society.

Students must learn how these key concepts of democratic political theory are institutionalized and practiced in their own country in comparison to other nation states around the world. Finally, students must pursue inquiries about transitional, generic, and perennial problems of any constitutional democracy, including how to combine: (1) Liberty with order, (2) Majority rule with minority rights, and (3) Private rights with the public good. Everyone must understand that a constitutional democracy will fail if: (1) The government has too much or too little power, (2) The government overemphasizes majority rule at the expense of minority rights or vice versa. (3) Having a weak civil society. How to address these issues practically and effectively is the ultimate challenge of citizenship in a constitutional democracy and the determiner of the political system's destiny.

CIVIC SKILLS

Citizens must effectively apply core knowledge to civic life if it is going to serve them well. Thus, a central facet of civic education for a constitutional democracy is the development of intellectual and participatory skills, which enable citizens to think and act on behalf of their individual rights and the common good. Intellectual skills empower citizens to identify, describe, and explain information and ideas pertinent to public issues and to make and defend decisions on these issues. Participatory skills empower citizens to influence public policy decisions and to hold their elected officials accountable for their actions. The development of civic skills requires active learning by students both inside and outside the classroom at home with their parents, family members, and friends. Students should be challenged to use information and ideas, individually and collectively to analyze case studies, respond to public issues, and resolve political, economic and social problems.

CIVIC VIRTUES

A third generic category of democratic civic education pertains to virtues. These are important character traits that individuals must have to sustain and improve a constitutional democracy. If citizens are to enjoy the privileges and rights of their polity, they must take responsibility for them. This requires a certain measure of civic virtue.

Civic virtues such as self-discipline, civility, compassion, tolerance, and respect for others are indispensable to the proper functioning of a civil society and constitutional government. These characteristics must be nurtured through social agencies, including schools, to ensure a healthy democracy.

Whenever we speak about the future of any society, we are really speaking about the youth and their prospects. In the case of any post-communist nation, preparing young people for better futures is one of the core obligations of the adult community. This means providing young people with the skills needed to prosper. There also exist qualities of character that determine the success or failure in a person's life. Foremost are the virtues that make possible a life of honor an integrity. Citizens of any country have the obligation to foster virtuous responsible citizenship in a free society is a crucial part of this obligation for adult citizens.

THE DEMOCRATIC TEACHER

As educational reformers in post-communist countries have build new education programs for their transitions to support democratic values, many have turned to the western world for assistance in overcoming an imposing array of obstacles left by the former system. These obstacles include the lack of classroom instructional materials and many teachers with a meager understanding of what a democracy is. They have no formal training in appropriate pedagogical techniques to teach such materials. There are three general components of a democratic civic education, which transcends political boundaries and cultures. They are: (1) Core concepts that denote essential knowledge, (2) Intellectual and participatory skills that enable practical application of civic knowledge, and (3) Virtues that dispose citizens to act for the good of their community.

The effective democratic teacher should develop lessons and learning activities for students that emphasize and incorporates the three generic components of civic education in a classroom environment compatible with the theory and practices of democracy and liberty. The democratic teacher should also emphasize interactive learning tasks in which students are challenged to take responsibility for the achievement of educational objectives. The democratic teacher encourages and protects free and open expression of ideas in an atmosphere of academic freedom and mutual respect without any fears of negative consequences.

Furthermore, the democratic teacher should establish and apply all classroom rules fairly according to the principles of equal protection and due process for each individual. The recognition of these signals will show that true liberty is inextricably bound to rules and that individual freedom depends upon an equitable rule of law for all members of the community. Finally, the democratic teacher should create a classroom environment in which the worth and dignity of each person is respected.

SAMPLE LESSON PLAN: THE CONSTITUTION

The objective of the lesson plan will be to have the students develop an awareness of the constitution by exploring what it is and why it is important.

Terms to know: (1) Citizens, (2) Congress, (3) Constitution, (4) President, (5) Laws, (6) Judges, (7) Rights, and (8) Rules.

Concepts to learn: What is a Constitution? A constitution is a set of fundamental customs, traditions, rules, and laws that set forth the basic way a government is organized and operated. What are the specific roles of the executive, legislative and judicial branches of government under a democratic system?

What is a citizen? Do citizens have any power or control over the government? If so, how do citizens exercise their powers? What rights and responsibilities do citizens have?

What are rights? Rights are moral or legal claims justified in ways that are generally accepted within a society or the international community.

Where do rights come from, and how do they relate to one another? Rights set individuals or groups apart from each other and entitle them to be treated in a particular way.

Who may hold rights? Rights can be held by individuals, classes or categories of individuals, or institutions.

Individual rights: The idea that each individual can hold rights reflect the belief that humans should be considered autonomous and self-governing. This includes the belief that each individual should possess certain fundamental rights, such as those to freedom of thought and conscience, privacy, and movement. The emphasis on the rights of individuals is reflected in natural that all persons are created equal, that they are endowed by God with certain unalienable rights, that among these are life, liberty, and the pursuit of happiness according to the philosophy of John Locke. The purpose of government is to protect those rights.

Political rights: This rights address political participation and also are granted by the constitution of the country. Examples are the right to vote and engage in political activity.

Economic rights: These include choosing to work one wants to do, acquiring and disposing of private property, entering into contracts, joining labor unions or professional organizations. Democratic countries consider economic rights associated with property ownership to be personal rights as well.

HOW CITIZENS PARTICIPATE

One of the most important rights of a citizen in a democracy is the right to participate in governing their communities and nation. Teachers should introduce the concepts on how individual citizens can make a difference in their communities. These are some examples on how citizens can participate:

(1) Looking for information in newspapers, magazines, and reference materials and judging its accuracy.

(2) Voting in elections at all levels.

(3) Participating in a political discussion.

(4) Trying to persuade someone to vote a certain way.

(5) Signing a petition.

(6) Wearing a button or putting a sticker in your car.

(7) Writing letters to elected officials.

(8) Contributing money to a political party or candidate.

(9) Attending meetings to gain information, discuss issues, or lend support.

(10) Campaigning for a candidate of your choice.

(11) Lobbying for laws that are of special interest.

(12) Demonstrating through marches, boycotts, sit-ins, or other forms of protest.

(13) Serving as a juror.

(14) Running for office.

(15) Holding public office.

(16) Serving your country through the military.

(17) Disobeying laws and taking the consequences to demonstrate that a law or policy is unjust.

CASE STUDIES

Three countries in particular are worth studying their success in developing and implementing their respective education transformations. As we will see, their reforms focused on providing training and skills for citizens of all ages in their respective development of their democratic system. These countries are the Czech Republic, Latvia and Poland.

CZECH REPUBLIC

The establishment of separate Czech and Slovak Republics on January 1, 1993 marked the start of separate democratic reform movements. After more than forty years with Soviet communist ideology as the central theme in teacher education and curriculum development, Czech educational reformers turned to various western resources for assistance in reforming civic education in their schools. The Center for Civic Education in California worked very closely with Czech reformers to establish national educational standards for the teaching and learning of civics and government. This project was funded by the United States Department of Education.

Briefly, the intent of the project was to revise existing social studies curricular framework for schools by taking particular aim at overarching objectives for civic education reform started in 1989. Those objectives included the elimination of Marxist-Leninist perspectives in the historical, philosophical, and social science content of the curriculum; the re-introduction of the study of religion into the curriculum; a renewed study of Czech history, culture, heritage, and geography; and a pedagogical shift from transmitting information to passive students to promoting inquiry and active leaning. Accompanying each lesson was a teacher's manual that presented a rationale teaching methods to be used for each lesson.

As originally designed, the project included as a core component a curriculum development workshop for teachers. The workshop provided training and practice for teachers on how to incorporate the objectives of each lesson into the curriculum. The other two components were a partnership program between teachers in the United States and Czech teachers and the evaluation of the product by both parties. The evaluation provided the opportunity to access the effectiveness of the program in a timely manner that allowed for necessary changes to be developed and implemented.

The curriculum development workshop met weekly on the University of Iowa Campus. A selected group of Czech teachers took part in the twelve week workshop that focused on developing a set of lessons based on active learning strategies that foster democratic skills and attitudes. The content of the lessons centered on five key concepts derived from existing social science curriculum. These were: (1) State and government policy, (2) Constitutional and local law, (3) Citizenship and human rights, (4) Free market economics, and (5) The Czech republic and the Global community.

By the end of the workshop, the Czech teachers had written sixty-one lessons on twenty topics related to both the civic education reform objectives and the five key concepts of the social studies curriculum noted earlier. These lessons introduced teaching strategies rarely practiced before in the Czech republic such as role playing, simulations, educational games, decision trees, civic writing, and cooperative learning. Additionally, some lessons highlighted content areas new to Czech social studies courses, including civic activism and the development of political parties.

Four years later (1993), the same teachers involved in the development of the new curriculum conducted follow-up workshops in the Czech Republic and invited educators from the United States to participate. The purpose of the workshop was to review, evaluate, and prepare new materials for schools. At the same time, Czech teachers and researchers conducted a workshop on the methods of data collection and analysis required for a systematic evaluation of the new lessons. This component of the project focused on an evaluation of knowledge, skill, and attitude outcomes commonly associated with living in a democracy.

Given how long the country had been under totalitarian communism, it is unreasonable to expect complete educational reform to result from one curriculum project. However, the new education reform represented the kind of project that combines the educational expertise of a developing democracy with the contextual understanding of a transitional democracy in an effort to reform civic education through civic participation at all levels of the education system. Czech teachers continue to implement new curricula for democratic citizenship. Hope for sustaining a democratic movement in the Czech Republic has become a reality.

LATVIA

Understanding the connection between well educated citizens and democratic well being, many Latvians decided to reform the existing curriculum and teaching methods of their schools. They replaced the Soviet-era courses on citizenship with new teaching materials and methods suitable for citizenship in a true constitutional democracy. They also looked to the west for assistance. It came initially from the World Federation of Free Latvians, an international organization that had nurtured the spirit of national independence and liberty during the Soviet occupation of the country.

It started with a civic education project. Financial support for the project was provided by the National Endowment for Democracy. The project started in 1993 with the intention of designing and developing materials for new courses in civic education for schools. The introductory courses emphasized the interaction of citizens with their new constitutional government. Courses were also developed on the institution of government and the rights and responsibilities of citizens in an institutional democracy. The teaching methods emphasized active learning instead of passive reception of information. The lessons required students to acquire and apply information and ideas rather than merely receive and repeat them. The teachers also required the use of high level cognitive operations in the organization, interpretation, and evaluation of subject matter. Work groups taught skills of democratic participation and decision making through role playing, simulations, and political problem solving skills. Accompanying materials included a teacher handbook on civics, a student handbook on civics as well, and testing materials.

From the beginning, the staff of the project considered the education of teachers a critical component of the program. Unless teachers understood the content and pedagogy of civic education for democracy, the core mission of the project would go unfulfilled. Therefore, starting in 1994, the project staff conducted more than one hundred seminars and workshops for teachers in schools throughout Latvia. More than eight hundred teachers participated in the workshops which were based on lessons and teaching methods in the first year. By 1996, civic education had become part of the teacher education preparation at all major universities in Latvia.

The project was extremely successful. Present and future challenges include further promotion and development of civic education throughout society that includes knowledge, skills, and attitudes necessary for effective and responsible citizenship in a democracy.

POLAND

One of the largest and most comprehensive projects of transition was the Education for Democratic Citizenship in Poland, a cooperative effort of the Polish Ministry of National Education in locally controlled schools in Warsaw. The project is often cited as a model of how to construct a long-term dimensional approach to civic education reform.

The project started in 1991, and its plan called for a set of distinct but related activities that would respond to specific, urgent problems identified by the Polish community, such as the desperate need for new teaching materials. The overall goals of the project were to institutionalize civic education in all schools in Poland.

The National Endowment for Democracy first funded a small project, which enlisted twenty-five Polish educators in developing curriculum guides and support materials. These guides presented the rationale, goals, objectives, and content outlines for primary and secondary school civic curriculum. For example, one supporting book presented sixteen sample lesson plans illustrating topics and goals set forth in the curriculum guide. A second book consisted of thirty-six readings on political life, citizenship, and human rights by prominent Polish scholars and political activists.

Another project worth noting was the Primary School Civic Course, funded by the Pew Charitable Trust. In this case, Polish university professors prepared detailed syllabus for a two semester course on the principles of democracy as they applied to the organization and operations of schools. The syllabus included goals, detailed explanations, suggested readings, and sample teaching strategies for the following topics. (1) Student's rights and responsibilities, (2)

Schools and the local community, and (3) The role of schools in a democratic society.

In late 1993, a group of prominent educators and scholars from across Poland met in Warsaw to discuss and critique the materials developed for these projects. The meetings were productive in the sense that new ideas were introduced, and the curriculum and teaching methods were adopted according to the needs of the rapidly changing Polish society. The program was very successful from the point of view of inter-grating individuals and organizations into a democratic society.

CONCLUSION

There are a number of lessons that can be learned from post-Soviet countries throughout Central and Eastern Europe that could apply to Cuba in the future. The education system of the Czech Republic was a frontrunner in playing an active role in the government's transition. In 2001, the government of the Czech Republic approved the National Programs of Development Education, a document that was part of their strategy to further expand social and economic development in the country. The focus of the plan was to develop human and social capital by focusing on the creation of a new value system that emphasized democratic citizenship and the quality of everyday life for the Czech citizens. This was the first project adopted by the new government after the political changes of 1989 to focus on systematic reform.

The strategy aimed to upgrade the level of education and human resource development across society with the purpose of creating a strong civil society that could sustain a democratic society for years to come. The creation of political and economic conditions for perpetual change in attitudes towards investment in education drove the plan. Each strategic concept was characterized by the implementation of a flexible system of lifelong learning aimed to educate children, youth, and adults to develop a civil society that could support a democratic form of government and a free economic system.

(1) The adaptation of an educational system that takes into consideration the everyday needs of society such as food, shelter and jobs. The goal was to increase the quality and practical function of the education system in preparation for the demands a new system will need to provide professional and technical training that it can develop individuals with employable skills who would sustain a developing economy.

(2) The development of a system that will monitor and evaluate the effectiveness of the plan. The idea was to monitor the input and output of the education system to assure that it was meeting the needs of the new citizens and government.

(3) The promotion of internal reforms and openness of the educational institutions call for an autonomous system that would allow each institution to experiment with new techniques. The system should also encourage collaborators between the public and private sectors along the lines of training, research, and new developments.

(4) The adaptation of the role and professional standards of the academic community should be geared towards financially supporting the design of programs to meet the needs of society to be coordinated with the business sector. The plan should also strengthen the social and professional status of teachers and academics.

(5) The transition from a centralized system of educational management to a decentralized and flexible system that can react to the needs of its citizens more quickly will be accomplished by enlisting the active participation of the public and private sectors of civil society in the process of planning, organizing, implementation and evaluation. Finally, it should have very specific accountability measures.

In summary, education reconstruction in a post-communist country will continue to face many obstacles including: (1) Physical reconstruction, (2) Ideological reconstruction, (3) Psychological reconstruction, (4) Provision of materials and curricular reconstruction, and (5) Human Resources.

The educational rehabilitation and reconstruction of the United Nations Educational, Scientific and Cultural Organization (UNESCO) speaks of reconstruction as a relatively protected process with short, medium, and long term goals. Emergency programs fulfill basic requirements needed to get the education system such as the one in Cuba working again. They respond to the most urgent human and material needs and manage human components. Post-communist countries must work with groups and individuals in order to determine priorities, as efforts will be directed towards first meeting the basic needs of the population. UNESCO for years has argues that states must not carry out reconstruction by piecemeal, but must carefully plan and implement it. Agencies concerned with reconstruction should be formulating plans for intervention in education long before it is possible to put such programs in place. However, it is very important to be aware that importing ideas and plans from another country might not work. Historical, cultural and human experiences should always be taken into consideration.

In terms of medium and long term reconstruction, UNESCO speaks of an education system master plan that will emerge from needs analysis based on the following dimensions and components. (1) Environmental, (2) Organizational, (3) Infrastructural, (4) Material and financial, (5) Human, (6) Institutional, (7) Pedagogical, and (8) Curricular.

Effective planning for all aspects of educational reconstruction and capacity building will depend on the creation of organizational frameworks at the national, local, and institutional levels.

The toughest challenges facing any post-communist country like Cuba in its transition will be (1) Ideological reconstruction, and (2) Psychological reconstruction. Though these two issues merit further exploration and research, they are key to building and sustaining a civil society.

Ideological reconstruction in the process of democratization is seen as a major factor in reforming authoritarian, totalitarian, and autocratic systems. It adjust the attitudes of individuals and encourages the replacement of previous structures, values and human behavior. Vital to democratizing education is the encouragement of critical, independent, and creative thinking. UNESCO strongly believes that to accomplish this task, the new education system in transition has two fundamental duties. The first is to educate children and adults with a sense of openness and comprehension toward other people, their cultures and histories, and their fundamental shared humanity. The second task is to teach them the importance of refusing violence and adopting peaceful means for resolving conflicts and disagreements.

A common feature of any post-conflict situation is the presence of various psychological problems ranging from demoralization to severe trauma. The need for fast psychological reconstruction has been recognized by a number of international agencies as a key to any form of successful transition that is accompanied by conflict.

In the confusion and deprivation that often characterizes post-crisis situations, it is not uncommon for those affected to experience lack of confidence, low morale, and frequent nostalgia. The reestablishment of morale and restoration of confidence is a difficult and trying process that often creates a feeling of nostalgia for past practices and lifestyles. In many post-Soviet bloc countries, teachers and students continued to find the implementation of unfamiliar new policies, practices, and learning styles difficult to cope with.

The uncertainty, insecurity, and instability that follow periods of crisis inevitably result in stress, anxieties, and depression conditions which often lead to physical illness in both children and adults. A widespread need will exists for special rehabilitation programs designed to assist children traumatized by the changes, especially those following violence or the loss of a family member as a result of conflict. Numerous examples of programs used by countries going through transition exist to help identify and treat trauma sufferers are available. However, it is important to recognize that psychological reconstruction, especially in the case of trauma, is a long term process. Trauma also represents a serious obstacle in the education process. Regular schooling is important in the establishment of the secure, caring environment deemed by psychiatrist and psychologist to be the most effective means of relieving psychological repercussions for children.

It is important in any transition to listen to individual needs and develop plans of action that are flexible and can be adapted to various ideological and psychological conditions. If this is not done from the beginning, then the transition process will be short lived and will eventually fail.

CHAPTER FIVE

FINAL THOUGHTS

The concept of transitions has been central to discussions of democratization for more than three decades. Transitions has been the primary term used to describe the political changed that typified what Samuel Huntington labeled the "third wave" of democratization. The birth of new democracies in well over fifty countries that have made democracy the most common form of government in the world today. The early days of transitions were the 1980's and 1990's particularly with the fall of the Soviet Union. By the turn of the twenty-first century, the birth of new democracies had slowed down, partly because so many countries had already adopted some form of democracy. As a result, political scientist turned their attention to issues of democratic consolidation, and then to the quality of democracies around the world.

The use of the word "transition" to refer to a change in political regimes is relatively new. Yet many scholars studying developing countries are still interested in the question of how much a democracy comes into being. The word "Transition" is defined by some scholars as the interval between one political regime and another which is not necessarily a democratic system. The emphasize on the path for transitions is one that is neither violent nor revolutionary but works through negotiations between the outgoing authoritarian regime and its opposition, and often relies upon formal or informal pacts or agreements that provide security guarantees to both sides.

Professor Francis Fukuyama said "democracy is a complex set of institutions that involves accountability, rule of law, and an adequate state." (48) All of these variables have to work in conjunction with one another for a successful democracy to develop and be able to institutionalize all of its components understanding that it will not happen over night. For this and other reasons, Professor Tom Carothers has call for an end to the transition paradigm, as he argues that many countries said to be undergoing a democratic transition are in fact stuck in what he calls the "Grey Zone" and therefore there are no guarantees that they will ever emerge as liberal democracies.

In the years leading up to the fall of the Soviet Union many scholars thought that the great alternative to the communist regimes would be a vibrant civil society. Twenty plus years after the dust of the Berlin wall has settled, many political scientist have argued that in 1989, civil society became a genuine sociological reality only in Poland, whereas in countries such as the Czech Republic, East Germany and Hungary, the "uncivil society" of the communist establishment still created and implemented the rules. There was no successful civil movement from below to counter the regimes of these countries. Instead, communist ruling elites collapsed as a result of their own failures. In other words, civil society in these countries did not defeat communism. Communism defeated itself. Will this be the case in Cuba?

Others have argued that had civil society not been present to undermine communism, there would never have been a collapsed of the system. Civil society meant not only the rediscovery of human autonomy, but also a search for a political movement rooted in morality.

When we look at Mikhael Gorbachev's *Perestroika,* he needed to restructure the country by giving the people a sense of responsibility for the country's destiny. The alienation that had been caused by the weakened ties between the government and society had to change. This became a very tough obstacle to overcome since their participation had been very limited. Gorbachev understood that he needed to address the basic needs of society immediately. His plan called for balancing the "changes" between the economic and social spheres. If the interests of society were disregarded for the sake of economic development alone, Russia's transition would not succeed.

Gorbachev understood that social changes would be difficult particularly among the young generation that wanted to see improvements immediately. His plan called for not eroding completely the existing values of Soviet society for the fear of causing a great deal of trauma particularly among the older generation. He later admitted that this was a mistake. After so many years under totalitarian-communist rule, Gorbachev underestimated the power and influence such value system had had on the people. He said in a speech that "the moral aspect was of tremendous importance. If the government did not attempt to revive the value of self, the changes of restructuring our system of government will fail. We can propose the right policies and effective mechanisms, but we will not accomplish anything if we do not improve the moral values of society. Above all social justice, distribution according to labor input, uniform discipline, laws, rules and requirements for all are necessary." (49). The problem was that it was too much for society to understand so quickly. Many feared what "change" would bring them.

As difficult as it was at the beginning to win the support of many sectors within the government and society, Gorbachev still believed that he still had enough support to implement his *Perestroika*. During this period of "change" Gorbachev worked very hard to win the support of the young people. He strongly believed that it would be their generation who would eventually be responsible for molding the future of Russia. Gorbachev's policies addressed many of the young generation's needs. These were the formative years of their lives regarding their personal futures, family, occupations, and political and civil involvement. The young people needed to be nurtured and encouraged to participate in the plans for "change" Gorbachev knew that the young generation no longer supported the Marxist-Leninist ideology. They also did not know what system of government their country was best suited for. Very similar to what the young generation in Cuba feels today. The failure of *Perestroika* left most of the young generation on Russia very apathetic towards those that govern Russia today and looking outside Russia for a better future.

To understand the diversity of post-communist transitions, we need to assess not only the weight of the dissident and opposition experience, but also the lingering influence of communist legacies. Communist parties fell from power, but not all their members fell with them. For example, Russia's Boris Yeltsin was a member of the communist nomenclature who claimed to have become a genuine democrat. We can find similar examples in Poland, Czech Republic, Hungary and others. In the case of Yeltsin, he was able to dismember the institutional bureaucracy of Leninist order but failed to create a robust democratic polity. The rise of Vladimir Putin, a mid-level KGB man plucked from obscurity and made heir-apparent to the Russian presidency by Yeltsin's inner circle of advisors and the triumph of

"Putinism" bear stark witness to the failure of Yeltsin's revolution and making Russia a democratic state.

In Central and Eastern Europe today, communism's collectivist and egalitarian promises have risen again in the form of new salvation fantasies that attempt to synthesize far-left and far-right visions. Frustrations and malaise are rampant, and demagogues, as before are to exploit them for their own cynical purposes. Some of these individuals have ties to the old regimes. People who had been informers or propagandists for the communist dictatorships have reinvented themselves as apostles of anti-western, anti-democratic ideologies, preaching for a return to fantasies of racial purity.

Looking at Russian today, we are reminded that a democratic polity in which the individual is treated decently and human rights are respected cannot be built on amnesia, mystification, imposture, lies and military aggression into other sovereign countries. The crucial underlying problem in Russia remains the symbol of Stalin and the way his ghost continues to haunt the collective memory and the public imagination of those that govern the country. Can this be the case in Cuba?

Putin's "democracy" is but in fact an authoritarian system with an eclectic and questionable constellation of ideological claims to the past. It is rooted precisely in a perpetuation of denial regarding communism and its depredations. Under Yeltsin there were inconclusive attempts to organize a civil society and a promise of a better Russia. Since then, Soviet mythologizing has ruled the day. This can very well happen in the not too distance future of Cuba.

To summarize, an established civil society based on a civic culture is in the theory of regime changes the last step of consolidation of a true democracy. However, a civil society is not necessarily the only outcome of the transformation to a democracy, but it is in different ways a stimulus of transformation itself (Crossant, Lawth, Mericel, 2000) (50). Then what is a civil society? I would say that it is an arena of polity where self-organization groups, movements, and individuals, relatively autonomous from the government, attempt to articulate values, create associations and solidarities to advance their interests. Then a normative theory of civil society has to include protection of the people against abuse of power by the state, mediation between the public and private sector, socialization, integration and open communication.

The theory of regime change enumerates the transformation process to democracy in three stages. Long time evolution, negotiated regime change, collapse of the autocracy, and bottom up changes in government, What will be the process in Cuba?

Over the last twenty years scholars have been studying models of transition that could apply to Cuba in the future. In reality, there is no single model that has worked anywhere 100 percent. The model that will apply to Cuba will come out of experiences, culture, and political and social environment Cubans have lived under for the last fifty-five years. The other part of the model will come from the informality pervasive in Cuban socialism and the "Politics of Affection" and dissatisfaction with a system that has maintain the Castro's in power. Will this model help Cuba's transition? Will "Lo Informal" facilitate or inhibit the "change"? Will the " Politics of Affection" contribute to the mass formation of civil society and democratization?

As I mentioned earlier in the book, I believe that in the long run, the political culture of passion, affection, dissatisfaction, and "Lo Informal" will have a contradictory impact Cuba's political transition. The "Politics of Passion" will exert its influence on governance and social life in a way that will undermine democratic norms, if democracy is to be established in Cuba someday. However, passion and affection are not exclusive to Cuban politics alone. On the contrary, emotions illuminate how people relate to the social and political order. We have witnessed it all over the world. Most recently in Egypt, Ukraine and Venezuela. Such values of behavior will always be present. It is up to each country's organized or unorganized civil society to channel those energies in ways that will bring positive "change" at the end. Cuba will be no different.

WORKS CITED

(1)   Speech by Fidel Castro to the Cuban National Assembly, 1991.

(2)   Damian Fernandez, *Cuba and the Passion of Politics.* pp. 65-70. 2000.

(3)   Damian Fernandez, Ibid. Pg. 68.

(4)   Jose Azel, *Manana in Cuba.* Pg. 70, 2010.

(5)   Juan Carlos Espinosa. *Civil Society in Cuba.* Paper Presented to the Association for the Study of the Cuban Economy, 2001.

(6)   Juan Carlos Espinosa, Ibid, 2001.

(7)   Anthony Smith, *The Origins of Nations,* pp. 201-205. 1998.

(8)   Weigle and Butterfield, *Civil Society in Reforming Communist Regimes.* Pp. 1-24. 1992.

(9)   Ariel Hidalgo, *Disidencia.* Ediciones Universal, 1994.

(10)   Wcigle and Butterfield, Ibid. pg. 98.

(11)   Rafael Hernandez, *Temas.* Cuban Journal Interview. 1991.

(12)   Fidel Castro. Speech to the International Book Fair in Havana, Cuba. 1997.

(13)   Pope John Paul II Speech in Havana, Cuba. 1998.

(14)   Gorky Aguila, Interview in Havana, Cuba 2002.

(15)   Damian Fernandez, Ibid, pg. 101.

(16)   Damian Fernandez, Ibid, pg. 171.

(17)   Ramiro Valdez Jr., Interview in Coral Gables, Fla. 2008.

(18)   Jorge Luis Garcia Perez " Antunez." Interview in Havana, Cuba. 2007.

(19)   Weigle and Butterfield, ibid. pg. 27.

(20)   C.C Hughes *Culture in Clinical Psychology. ,pp 221-226. 1976.*

(21)   C. C. Hughes ibid, pg. 225.

(22)   Kluckhorn, F.R. & Strobeck, F.L. *Variations in Value Orientations,* 19961.

(23)   Yoani Sanchez, Speech at the Institute for Cuban and Cuban-American Studies, University of Miami. Spring, 2012.

(24)   G. Smith, *The Psychological Dimensions of Transition.* Pg. 135. 1999.

(25)   E.S. Shiraev. *Generational Adaptation to Transition.* Pg. 102. 1999.

(26)   Ian Bremmer. *The J Curve.*

(27)   Wieckzorkowska, G. and E. Burstein. *Monitoring Social Adaptation to Change.* Pp. 155-172. 2001.

(28)   W.S. Wooden. *Youth Culture in Post Soviet Cuba,.* Pp 132-150. 2002.

(29)   A, Inkeles & R. Bauer. *Daily Life in a Totalitarian*

(30)   C. Roberts. *Measuring Cuban Public Opinion.* Paper presented to the Association for the Study of the Cuban Economy. 1999.

(31)   Roberts. Ibid. pg. 23. 1999

(32)   Juan Tamayo, Article in the Miami Herald, January, 2014.

(33)   Damian Fernandez, Ibid. pg 57.

(34)   Milton Carrow. *Democracy, Social Values and Public, 1998.*

(35)   Inglehart, 1977.

(36)   Damian Fernandez, Iid, pg 22. Cuban Transition Project.

(37)   Damian Fernadez, Ibid 22. Cuban Transition Project.1997.

(38)   Damian Fernandez, Ibid. pg. 27.

(39)   Damian Fernandez., ibid, pg. 22. Cuban Transition Project. Pp. 19-25.

(40)   Damian Fernandez, ibid, pg. 27.

(41)   Joseph Colomer, *Strategic Transitions.* Pp..35,n2002.

(42)   Cesar Birzea. *Educational Policies of the Countries in Transition., 1994.*

(43)   Cesar Birzae Educational. Policies of The Countries in Transition.

(44)   Oxford Studies in Comparative Education. 1995.

(45)   Benigno Aguirre, Ibid. 1994.

(46)   Thompson, 1990.

(47)   Andy Gomez, *The Role of Education in a Developing Nation.* Cuban Transition Project. ICCAS. 2002

(48)   Francis Fukuyama. *Trust. 1995.*

(49)   Mikhael Gorbachev, *Perestroika, 1987.*

(50)   Crossant, Lawth, Mericel. 2002.

REFERENCES

Bruhn, J. G. (1994), Psychological Adaptation to Rapid Societal Change in Poland. Polish Review Bulletin, 25(3), 153-161.

Bernal, G. (1982). Cuban Families. In M. McGoldrick, J. K. Pierce & J. Giordano (eds), Ethnicity and Family Therapy (pp. 187-207). New York; Guilford Press

Birzea, Cesar. 1994. Educational Politics in the Transition Period. Comparative Education. 31: 141-159.

Clark. J. (1982). Documento de Consulta (Monografia). Encuentro INternacional de Comunidades de REflexion Eclesial en la Diaspora. Miami, Fla. Catholic Archdiocese of Miami.

Conde. Y. M. (1999) Operacion Pedro Pan: The Untold Exodus of 14,948 Cuban Children. New York; Rutledge.

Corral, O. (2004, March 11). Poll: Hardline on Cuba Endures. The Miami herald, pp 3B.

Deming, W.E. (1943). Statistical Adjustment of Data. New York. Dover.

Elliott, A, & Del Valle, E. (2003, February 12). Cuban eXiles Shifting Hardline Position. The Miami Herald, pp. A1-A2.

Fernandez, Damian. Cuba and the Passion of Politics, University of texas Press. 2000.

Gmech, G. (1980). Return Migration. Annual rEview of Anthropology, 9, 135-159.

Gorbachev, Mikhael. Perestroika, Harper & Row 1987.

Hughes, C. C. (1993). Culture in Clinical Psychiatry. In A. Gaw (Ed), Culture, Ethnicity and Mental Illness (pp.221-226). Washington DC. American Psychiatry Press.

Hughes, C. C. (1976). Custom made: Introductory Readings in Cultural Anthropology. Chicago. Rand McNally.

Inclan, J. (1985). Variations in Value Orientations in Mental Health Networks. Psychotherapy, 22, 54-59.

Inkeles, A. & Bauer, R. (1968). The Soviet Citizen: Daily life in a Totalitarian Society. New York. Atheneum.

KLuckhohn, F. R. & Strodbeck, F. L. (1961) Variations in Value Orientations. Evanston, Il; Row-Peterson.

Lewis, O. (1966). La Vida: Living in a Culture of Poverty. New York; Random House.

Little, R. & Wu, M. M. (1991). Models for contingency Tables with known Margins When target and sampled population. Journal of the American Statistical association, 86, (413), 87-95.

Montaner, C. A. (2002). Cuba: Un Siglo de Doloroso Aprendizaje . Univerity of Miami, Institute for Cuban and Cuban-American Studies.

Mostaller, F. (1968). Association and Estimation in Contingency Tables. Journal of the American Statistical association, 63, (321), 1-28.

Nackerud, L., Springer, A., Larrison, C. & Issac, A. (1999). The End of the Cuban Contradiction. The International Migration Review. 33, (1), 176-193.

Oppenheimer, A. (2001, December 4). Confrontation Policy a Flop. The Miami Herald, pp. B1-B2.

Pumariaga, Andres J. & Rothe, Eugenio. The Mental Health of Immigrants and Refugees. Community Health Journal. Vol. 41, #5, October, 2005.

Polyzoi, E. Fullan, M. & Anchan, J. P. (eds). Change Forces in Post-Communist Eastern Europe: Education in Transition. New York: Routledge Falmer.

Roberts, C. (1999, August). Measuring Cuban Public Opinion: Methodology. Association for the Study of the Cuban Economy.

Schopflin, George. Politics in Eastern Europe: 1945-1992. Oxford, Blackwell, 1993.

Wooden, W.S. Escamilla, A. 7 Antoniuk, S. (2002). Youth Culture in Post-Communist Cuba. National Social sCience Journal. 18(2), 132-150.

www.ingramcontent.com/pod-product-compliance
Lightning Source LLC
Chambersburg PA
CBHW020538290526
45786CB00002B/937